The Art Activity Manual

A Groupwork Resource

Marylyn Cropley

Speechmark

First published in 2004 by
Speechmark Publishing Ltd, Telford Road, Bicester, Oxon OX26 4LQ, UK
www.speechmark.net

© Marylyn Cropley, 2004

002-5141 / Printed in the United Kingdom/1010

British Library Cataloguing in Publication Data
Cropley, Marylyn
    The art activity manual : a groupwork resource
    1. Art therapy – Handbooks, manuals, etc. 2. Social group work
    I. Title
    615.8'5156

ISBN 0 86388 431 8

Contents

Introduction

The Art Activity Manual offers skills-based activities with therapeutic outcomes. It aims to assist group facilitators working with adults with learning disabilities, physical disabilities, sensory loss, mental health needs and older people. This book can also be used independently by individual artists, self-help art groups and group facilitators working with children. It offers several approaches to enable people to explore the world of art and seek the 'artist within', through inspiring and non-threatening activities. It does not set out to teach art skills, nor to present therapeutic interventions in a formal sense: rather, it offers a flexible, non-prescriptive approach for group facilitators and members to explore and develop their own style and technique, within a general appreciation of art.

The activities call on the resources and abilities people already have, while further developing their art skills and knowledge. Many of the sessions can be adapted to meet individual needs, and develop a person-centred approach to art and communication. Art is universally shared in some form or another. Every person has the ability to be creative and expressive, given encouragement, support and opportunity. Adults with disabilities hold within them a wealth of lifetime experiences, feelings and values that can be expressed and shared through art.

Within every person is an artist waiting to be discovered, or an art lover looking to be inspired or delighted. The ultimate aim of this book is to allow people to be creative, and to appreciate and challenge self and others in their own time and in their own way, without the boundaries and constraints of a predetermined, and often judgemental, art world.

Rationale behind this Book

Over the years, art has been a powerful intervention and communication tool for people, with or without a disability. Books, videos, teaching plans and instructions on learning specific skills and techniques, famous artists, styles, self-development and art therapy are now widely available. Indeed, the amount of information can appear to be rather daunting to facilitators, confused as to where to begin or where to look next. Much time is spent researching ideas and information to put together session plans which meet the needs of the group, cover important elements in art, and also develop a progression of experiences that offers a journey through the world of art in practical, informative ways at basic levels.

This book offers a starting point. It consolidates a collection of activities and projects, the essence of which has been used successfully by artists as individuals, or in groups, time and time again. *The Art Activity Manual* offers an approach to art that is practical and non-prescriptive. It enables artists to explore and discover their own level of skills, style and preferences, and encourages them to speak and decide for themselves. Thus it avoids people saying they like something when they do not, just to please others – the 'emperor's new clothes' syndrome, so often found amongst artists lacking the courage of their own convictions.

This resource book is about doing and enjoying, rather than achieving specific standards and skills. It aims to integrate an ordinary interest in art with specialist considerations. The ultimate intention is for facilitators and groups, rather than the author, to determine how the book will be used. Incorporating a simple, practical and modern approach to art, including the use of computers, it also considers presentation and exhibiting of work to celebrate the endeavours and achievements of group members as artists. It caters for the growing requirements for facilitators to find fast, efficient, and cost-effective ways to meet individual needs within group settings.

How to Use this Book

Before using the book, it is a good idea to become familiar with its contents and overview. Identify the needs and wishes of the group where possible. What are their desired outcomes?

The Art Activity Manual is structured in three parts:
* **Part I** offers ideas and preparation for group activities.
* **Part II** provides a series of session plans that cover a period of 15 weeks, each session lasting approximately one hour. There are three options to choose from in most sessions, giving the facilitator flexibility to select a programme to suit the needs of the group. The contents of the session plans cover basic elements in art – for example, colour and shape, composition, drawing and painting, and making prints. It includes main categories, such as flora and fauna, environment, human, abstract, spiritual and fantasy.

✳ **Part III** presents project ideas that further inspire and motivate the group facilitator and members. The layout is the same as that of the session plans, and offers ideas and suggestions that can be adapted by the facilitator to produce more session plans or to be used as 'one off' projects. For example, the project on 'The Four Seasons' could last a whole year. Other topics covered are relevant and important to everyday needs and experiences. These range from the five senses, spirituality and communication, to the exploration of art, both old and new. Ideas for further activities may arise from the projects, and it is worth making a note of these to develop the scope and use of this book.

The Art Resource Box, mentioned in most session plans, is symbolic, and represents the holding and storage of art materials needed for the activities. It can be one or several portable or stationary containers. The 'You Will Need' list in Part I offers a versatile list of materials to store in the Art Resource Box.

It helps to allow time to find or purchase resources before the sessions begin. It is advisable for the facilitator to try out the activities beforehand, to enable a confident, practical and realistic presentation that meets both the facilitator's and members' requirements and levels of ability.

This book is not designed to teach art in a formal way. It offers opportunities to enable and support people to explore the use of, and experiment with, art materials, and to enjoy experiences through art. If, however, someone wishes to develop skills further, and needs information on art classes or other learning opportunities, it is well worth exploring other courses and support available in the local community to harness new-found enthusiasm.

When offering discussion and evaluating work in sessions, try to encourage people to remain constructive, and avoid comparisons. At the same time, respect and validate people's views and opinions. There is no 'right' or 'wrong' way to practise art, unless someone chooses to define this and others choose to follow. It is important to enable artists to decide for themselves how they are progressing, and to own a style or experience with confidence and conviction.

How this Book will Benefit the Group Facilitator

The Art Activity Manual encourages facilitators to stretch beyond their personal boundaries and explore other areas in art. They will work with individuals or groups in a fun, flexible and dynamic way. The facilitator need not be competent in art, or trained in therapeutic interventions: enthusiasm, creativity, and eagerness to participate and explore alongside others are the important qualities. Over 100 ideas and suggestions, with session or project plans, are set out in detail. The facilitator will not be short of ideas for quite some time! New ideas may also emanate from the group and facilitator, once the activities begin.

Sessions and projects combine to offer a journey across the world of art, and a self-discovery adventure to seek the 'artist within'. The facilitator, as well as the group, will reap the benefits. The approach is practical and experiential, and assists facilitators to support people with mixed abilities and levels of need. The group facilitator can offer additional learning through art – for example, improving communication skills, building confidence and self-esteem, and developing self-awareness. The activities use the minimum of resources and focus mainly on the participants, encouraging (and enabling) facilitators to be resourceful and economical. They will find ways to work within a limited budget, at times when resources and funding are scarce.

Ideas offer ways to recycle people's work, as well as using recycled resources. The Art Resource Box is designed to use materials that are known, easily obtainable and fairly economical. Activities are included to assist the facilitator to exhibit finished work and develop evaluations and plans for future work, as well as gaining a sense of achievement for themselves and the group. Facilitators will need to 'roll up their sleeves' and work alongside others. They will also need to be prepared to seek new resources, and to improve their own skills, knowledge, confidence and motivation.

PART I

Preparation

Meeting Needs

To meet the needs of a group, spend time 'getting to know' the participants. Clarify expectations, fears, and desired outcomes at the start. Cultivate a person-centred approach to activities, where each person is encouraged to say what they want, how they will achieve this, and what support they need, if any. (This is not always easy to do, especially with large groups, and where people are indecisive!) This book does not specify group numbers: the facilitator will need to decide this, although an ideal number would be up to six people. If more, split the group, and plan carefully to ensure that everyone participates in some way. Arrange additional help, if possible. Facilitators experienced in working with vulnerable adults may have a routine when catering for special needs within their groups. Getting to know group members, their support-networks and access to special resources, all help to identify and meet needs. Keeping notes on what is needed will ensure that no one is left out or forgotten.

These may be obvious comments on meeting needs, but it is surprising how quickly some things are forgotten, among the other concerns in setting up a group. Group members are artists: see the person and the 'artist' first, not the disability. Meeting special needs means identifying and using resources to enable someone to participate as fully as possible alongside others in the group. This could mean the purchase or adaptation of special equipment, one-to-one support from another person, access to buildings and workspaces, transport, medical or behavioural management, coping strategies, or more information/ awareness on a given disability.

Talk with individuals or carers to understand and identify any support needed. Look to the person's immediate network of family, friends and carers. Some may assist with activities or transport, or know a person who can. Ask individuals if they have equipment at home that they wish to bring in, or work with an individual and the occupational therapist or physiotherapist for ideas/resources. Before visiting public places or outdoor venues, check access and disability facilities, and keep a note of additional resources to take. Some organisations expect group facilitators to identify transport and human resource needs, and the ways in which these aspects of groupwork are to be funded. Ideally, people attending the groups pay for themselves. This may not always be easy for those on

benefits or lower income. If you need to, research and apply for local grants and funding – if you do not try, you will not get it!

Find out if there are partnership enterprises with other local artists, societies, schools, colleges or art councils, to enable group members to participate in community events. Why should artists with a known disability lose out on art activities happening in their own community? Encourage people to take responsibility for their own resources, art materials and choices, and involve them in the preparation and clearing up of activities. Discover how people communicate best, and use your findings to enhance teamwork and participation within the group. Value and respect differences – for example, of ability, attitudes, culture and background, and in beliefs and views on art – and use the knowledge, skills, expertise and talents within the group.

Avoid making assumptions. Respect and value confidences and privacy, and encourage participation, but do take 'no' for an answer! Be aware of your own prejudices and those of others. Accept that people have prejudices, but do not allow this to create hurtful or unhealthy attitudes within the group, or result in less favourable treatment for some members. Strive to be warm, honest, humorous and constructive. Seek to enjoy the activity. Aim for a relaxed and fun atmosphere, to achieve a therapeutic outcome: artists can be vulnerable, with or without a disability. Building confidence, self-esteem, and a genuine appreciation of art is the ultimate goal. However, 'a horse can be taken to water, but not made to drink', so offer opportunities with enthusiasm and commitment, but let the artist, own the outcome.

Aims and Objectives

The Art Activity Manual aims to offer art opportunities and practical activities, mainly through fine art experiences. It enables a journey through basic elements of art and everyday experiences. The ultimate aim is to facilitate a pathway for artists with disabilities or limited art opportunities to experience and value the benefit of art in general, and to find the 'artist within', either as a practical participant or a 'spectator'.

Each session or project has its own aim and method. However, the group facilitator or individual may want to add their own, or seek a different outcome to an activity. It is not compulsory to work to the aims in this book, or achieve them as described. Doing, participating, and enjoying the journey of self-awareness as an artist are the most important factors.

Planning and Evaluation

The planning for each session or project has already been done in this book. Each activity can be evaluated at the end if required. Evaluation gives facilitators and group members an opportunity to discover what benefits and desired outcomes have been gained from their experiences, and to identify any further action needed. Session 15 in Part II offers two options on evaluation. When planning for groups, it may be helpful to consider the following points:

* Know the group; clarify and agree needs and expectations
* Know the activity/project, and the resources needed, well. For example, where will it take place? What is the workspace like? How will people get there?
* Obtain resources, adequate storage, and funding as needed
* Research information and ideas, well before workshops start
* Collect as much information as possible on art in general
* Collect recycled resources to save on time and minimise costs
* Involve group members when making some decisions and preparing for activities
* Ask group members to bring in information and their own materials where possible – this not only saves on costs, but also encourages individuality and independence
* Have contingency plans, in case original plans fall through. Build a list of possible alternatives, such as places to visit, and have other workshops and resources available for use.

Presenting, Displaying and Storing Work

Not every artist wishes to show or even store their own work. While it is worth encouraging people to save their work, it is also important to respect and validate their views if they choose not to. Art can be a very private area for individual artists, and what they choose to do with their work must be their choice. On the other hand, many artists secretly, if not overtly, crave recognition and admiration for their achievements – or, at the very least, want to share what they have created with others. It is equally important to validate, value and celebrate completed work. So many vulnerable adults have created hundreds of artworks in different ways, only to have them stored away for years, and then rediscovered and thrown away, long after the artists themselves have moved on. It is a sad waste of talent and finished work.

Enable group members to take responsibilty for their own work: they must be the ones to decide its destiny – to throw away, store, take home, frame or participate in an exhibition. Do not store work for them. Be firm! If someone appears keen but too timid to exhibit, find alternative ways for them to achieve this initially, such as displaying the work in their bedroom, or another room at home, or by building up a private portfolio. Gradually build on this to increase confidence and courage to value and share their own work with others.

Part II, Session 14, offers options for presenting, storing and displaying work.

Risk Assessment/Health and Safety

Taking risks is part of common everyday experience for us all, including artists. In most cases, basic 'life' rules are observed and obeyed, instincts are followed, and common sense prevails. Modern technology has also improved tools and materials used by artists to minimise risk to health and safety. As a general rule, people take responsibilty for their own actions. This is especially so for artists, who choose which materials they use and the places they visit – for example, sketching outdoors on a cold windy day, by the edge of a cliff, perched on a wobbly stool, with no coat, licking brushes after using lead paint!

However, working with vulnerable adults calls for additional responsibility, rules and guidelines: completion of a risk assessment exercise is recommended. (If working for an organisation, follow its specific guidelines for doing risk assessments.) Risk assessment, although time-consuming and daunting, can be an asset to the facilitator. It can eliminate health and safety worries and stumbling blocks, or achieve safe outcomes for the facilitator and group, as well as giving strength to negotiations for resources, funding, and support. Although risks cannot be eliminated altogether – indeed they can be a healthy challenge – the activities and materials suggested in this book are designed to minimise risks and highlight caution where relevant.

It is the responsibilty of every participant to exercise caution when in a potential risk situation. It is important to raise health and safety issues with the group, and encourage individuals to take responsibilty for their actions. Work together to identify hazardous resources and the appropriate safety precautions needed in activities. Look for ways to identify and manage risk, rather than be overprotective.

Practical Hints and Tips

Experienced group facilitators may already have a 'list' of hints and tips: it is memorised and used automatically, or written somewhere 'in a safe place'. For those who are new facilitators, it is well worth beginning a personal list, as it can save time and trouble in the long run. Always keep a notebook nearby. Preparation and knowledge of group and activity goes a long way to achieving satisfactory outcomes. Try to visualise the activity from beginning to end, based on circumstances, and leave out or add elements to the plan as required.

As far as possible, prepare the workspace and resources before people turn up – keeping a detailed checklist of what is needed is helpful, in this respect – or involve the group in the preparation, allowing extra time to do this. Be prepared to improvise and adapt, before, during and after the activity. Do not worry if resources identified are not available or the budget is tight: the group members are the main resource. Have a discussion group instead of a practical activity, or ask people to bring in things to talk about. Session plans in this book offer hints and tips in the 'Alternatives' and 'Comments' sections. How useful they are will depend on the occasion, the style of facilitator, and the needs of the group. It is more relevant to develop a list while researching and preparing for activities, and from hindsight and evaluations.

Make it possible for people to participate in a practical way, even if this means copying, tracing, and photocopying work – 'Practice makes perfect'. However, be aware of copyright issues. Do not copy or sell anyone's work without their permission. Make group members aware of copyright guidelines and issues as they arise.

Keep the Art Resource Box topped up! It is very tempting to put off reviewing stock, but equally frustrating when the materials are not there when needed. Allow sufficient time to obtain alternate resources if necessary. Have a contingency plan for days when people do not want to participate, or things do not go to plan. Videos on art topics (good for splitting large groups), or ready-made colouring books for people to doodle or colour in, are useful in these situations, when the artist is unmotivated or lethargic! Recycling materials is a challenge, and an exciting element for an artist to work with, so try to use recycled materials frequently. For example, paint over canvas (if work is unwanted!) with emulsion or acrylic paint, and use it again; cut up and use unwanted work or paper for collage; keep old candles for wax resist painting;

use nature for colour, literally – 'paint' with grass by rubbing fresh grass on paper, and do the same with flowers, tree bark or burnt wood. Raid the kitchen for unwanted food, such as tea or coffee, and use it to 'paint' with. Unwanted make-up, nail varnish, household paints and fabric dyes can be interesting to try. Remember that some of these substances may be harmful, and precautions need to be taken.

Keep found and unwanted objects that may be useful as tools or alternatives to brushes – for example, feathers, twigs, lollipop sticks, knitting needles or cotton buds. Have a clear out regularly, and throw away what is not needed in the near future. It can be quite daunting when things pile up or, worse, the manager or a colleague take matters into their own hands, and decide to throw things out without consulting the facilitator or group!

Materials

In *The Art Activity Manual*, every session and project plan has a resource list to assist in the planning and preparation for each activity. It is neither prescriptive, nor set in stone. The group facilitator or individual artist should decide which resources to use. The 'Art Resource Box' dominates the resource list throughout the book. This is symbolic for storage space (either portable or static) that holds the basic materials needed for all the activities. If this is kept topped up, the sessions should run more smoothly.

The Art Resource Box can be a collection of stacking boxes, trolleys, or cupboards on wheels. Alternatively, it can be a permanent set of cupboards and drawers within or near a regular workspace. A list of materials is offered here for the contents of the Art Resource Box. It is up to the facilitator to purchase and select the preferred make or type of materials, depending on availability and the budget they have to work with. Seek guidance, if needed, from local art suppliers, artists, colleagues or mail-order firms. Look in art books to gain more detailed information on specific materials.

The Art Resource Box: Suggested Contents
* Pencils: 'hard' and 'soft' grades, watercolour pencils, pencil crayons
* Pens: ink pens, permanent markers, felt-tip pens
* Brushes: a selection, to include long-handled and large household paint brushes
* Paints: watercolour, gouache, poster, and acrylic; optional oil paints

* Pastels, chalk, oil-, conté- and charcoal-sticks
* Sharpeners, rubbers, rulers, hole punch, stapler, paper-clips (large), pairs of compasses
* Scissors, craft knives
* Sticky tape, masking tape, double-sided tape, BluTack®, glue sticks, Velcro® strips (self-adhesive), PVA glue (Polyvinyl Acetate white glue – lots of it, preferably in bottles to pour!), tacks
* Paper: (black, white, multi-coloured and different sizes) drawing paper, tissue paper, tracing- and carbon-paper, blotting paper, watercolour- and acrylic-paper, wallpaper, plenty of newspapers and magazines
* Card and mount boards: black, white, colours, different sizes
* Sketchbooks, ring binder files, clear sleeves
* Water, soap, towels, kitchen rolls, aprons, gloves, bins
* Optional: canvas on frames, easels, wooden boards, silk paints, glass paints, inks
* Boxes to collect recycled and 'found' materials, junk for art, collage materials and information

Many of the sessions suggest that the group facilitator makes use of books, videos and other sources of written or visual information to stimulate ideas and discussion. Use the local library – or perhaps the resources of a local college – as much as possible to keep costs down. For a small charge, libraries will usually order books/videos not immediately available on their shelves. The internet, galleries, discount stores, charity shops and art bookshops, as well as members of the group itself, are all valuable resources.

PART II

Session Plans

Introduction

Aims

To enable group members to:

* **Discuss the topic of art, and explore what art means to them individually**
* **Share different views on art, and discover a diversity of opinions on what art means to people**
* **Get to know each other.**

Materials

* **A variety of books about art and artists**
* **Small art objects – for example, sculptures, jewellery, pottery**
* **Pictures showing 'art' in the community – for example, graffitti, posters, adverts, architecture**
* **Anything else you can think of!**

Method

Lay out the pictures, books and art objects around the room, on tables, walls or display boards. Encourage people to wander around the room to look at the work, and handle it where possible. Ask each person to select a piece that they think is a 'work of art'. Choose one yourself. Allow each person to talk about the piece they have chosen, encouraging them to describe what they see, and why they think it is 'art'. If necessary, be the first to start. Have a general discussion about the group's understanding of art. Does everyone feel the same way? What are the differences of opinion? Create a group definition of 'art'.

Discussion – 'What is Art?' *(cont'd)*

Alternatives

1 Use pictures, symbols, or single-word flashcards to assist with communication, if necessary.

2 Show the group videos on art exhibitions or artists, and use them as a starting point for a discussion of 'art'.

3 Take the group to local art exhibitions or places of interest, and ask them to make a note of any 'works of art' they see. Use this work as a starting point for a discussion, following the visit.

4 Look at how adverts are made. Is art used in advertising, and how? What effect does this have on group members? Will they buy the product because of this? Encourage group discussion.

5 Look at nature. Is it a 'work of art'? Discuss. Use videos, photographs and books to inspire a creative atmosphere. Visit gardens, countryside, parks, etc.

Comments

If verbal communication is limited, encourage people to draw or paint randomly, and briefly discuss whether what they have achieved is a 'work of art'.

Aims

* **To enable group members to get to know each other, and enjoy the experience**
* **To encourage group members to create and explore images using various art media, collectively and spontaneously**
* **To demonstrate to group members that art experience can be shared by all, and that each person can 'make a mark' to create a piece of artwork.**

Materials

* **Art Resource Box**
* **Large rolls of wallpaper/lining paper**
* **Tape recorder and tape of relaxing music.**

Method

Spread out large sheets of paper on the tables where people are seated. Play the music, and encourage group members to listen for a minute or two. While the music is playing, demonstrate how members can 'make a mark' on the paper in front of them, by using the paint and other materials available – for example, make some marks by drawing circles, squiggles and doodles.

Ask group members to have a go, and assist where necessary. Encourage the group to work continuously, making marks, lines and shapes using materials and media of their choice. Without pressure, suggest that people move around the room if possible, adding to each other's work or linking pieces of work together. Continue this activity for 20–30 minutes. Approximately 15 minutes before the session closes, observe and celebrate the work by making positive comments and observations, encouraging the group to participate. Discuss ways to display the work as a whole or in fragments. Decide together when, and how, this will take place.

Alternatives

1 Instead of using paints and drawing materials, have group members use PVA glue and collage materials (patterned and colourful paper, fabric, natural found objects, pictures, tissue paper, as well as collectable items such as stamps and cards).

2 Place large sheets of paper around the room, as well as on the table. Encourage people to move around the room 'making a mark' randomly on different sheets of paper.

3 Have a theme to the exercise – for example, 'animals', 'trees', 'colours', 'shapes', 'people' or 'places'.

4 Encourage group members to cut up work into smaller pieces, and create mosaics and patterned pictures from these.

Comments

Try to create a non-judgemental atmosphere, in which members feel uninhibited. Encourage conversation around the work, or allow group members to work quietly while they are listening to the music. Let the group members take the lead. Work outdoors if it is a fine day.

Aims

* **To offer a relaxed and fun session, which enables group members to meet for the first time and enjoy each other's company**
* **To encourage people to create images in a non-threatening environment**
* **To enable people to use observation and concentration skills, and to be challenged in a light-hearted way through art.**

Materials

* **Large sheets of paper, or a flip-chart on a stand**
* **Something to attach paper to walls – place the paper where all the group members can see it at one time**
* **Charcoal, or large pens/wax crayons with which to draw**
* **A collection of simple line drawings, pictures, objects in carrier bags, or single words on flashcards, from which to draw/copy**
* **A tray on which to place the items, with a cloth to cover them**
* **Egg-timer, or watch with a second hand.**

Method

When preparing the room, place the collection of line drawings, objects and pictures on a table, away from where the group will work, and preferably in the next room. Begin by explaining to the group what is about to happen. Someone needs to start by drawing an image on the sheet of paper, slowly. (Ask someone to volunteer, but be prepared to start the drawing if no one offers!) The rest of the group must try to guess what the image will be *before it is completed*. The first person to guess correctly takes the next turn, or chooses the next person. Reassure people that the image does not have to be perfect – in fact, the less perfect it is, the harder it will be for the others to guess!

People can draw from imagination, or choose a line drawing or object to inspire them. Do this by taking the person to the table nearby or into the other room, and help them to select an appropriate prop from the collection laid out. If they feel unable to memorise and draw the item chosen from memory, place it on a tray covered with a cloth, and tell the person they can refer to this discreetly as and when needed, with your help. Time each 'turn' with the egg-timer or watch. (Agree a time limit with the group before you start.)

Alternatives

1 If someone does not want to participate by drawing, they can talk about the picture/object chosen, without showing this to the group or giving away too soon what it is they are holding.
2 Invite group members to close their eyes while someone describes the picture or object verbally. Encourage people to 'draw' the image in their mind and try to guess what it is.
3 Ask group members to take it in turns to have a go at 'drawing' an image in the air, and encourage the others to guess what it might be. These actions will encourage people to use large movements when drawing, and stretch their powers of imagination.

Comments

Encourage people to help each other where needed, or to work in teams, and try to create a competitive but non-threatening atmosphere: a sense of humour comes in handy here! For example, someone could select a picture/object, and another can do the drawing. Give points or prizes to teams.

The World of Art

Aims

To enable group members to:

* **Explore the world of art, in order to gain an understanding of what they like and dislike**
* **Form personal opinions and views on art, and to feel confident in expressing these views assertively**
* **Approach art with an open mind, and learn to evaluate work from objective and subjective viewpoints.**

Materials

* **Visual and tactile resources showing a variety of artwork – choose resources to meet the ability of group members**
* **Provide examples of paintings, architecture and sculpture, that range from prehistoric to modern times. (Include various cultures, such as Native American, African, Western, European and Far Eastern art.)**
* **A large sheet of paper, and felt-tip pens.**

Method

Spread the books, photographs and objects on a long table on one side of the room. If you are using videos or slides, arrange the room so that everyone seated can see the screen comfortably. Spend time with the group initially by looking through the resources chosen, and watching any video/slides offered.

Ask the group to select two pieces of artwork, one they dislike and one they like. Encourage people to think about why they like or dislike the works chosen. Set a 'ground rule' that each person must be allowed to speak freely, and not be judged by others. Place the two pictures chosen by the group on a wall or display board. Stick a large sheet of paper next to each picture, and write the appropriate title on each sheet – 'like' on the sheet next to the picture the group likes, and 'dislike' next to the picture they say they dislike. Then invite group members to talk about the pieces they have chosen, and say what they like or dislike about the work, and why. (Remind the group about the ground rule!)

While people are expressing their opinions, write down any words that describe how they feel about the items chosen on the large sheet of paper under the relevant headings. When everyone has contributed, have a general conversation on how the group felt about the choices. Were they surprised? Did they agree with the minority/majority of choices made? Were they swayed by others' views at any time? How assertive did they feel when having their say? Allow group members to talk freely about what they see.

Alternatives

1   If verbal communication is limited within the group for any reason, find a way to exhibit the artwork chosen by some group members, instead of holding a discussion. You could have a space to show the work people disliked separately from the work they liked. Use symbols and single words written on cards to describe comments made by the group. Place these near the relevant pieces of work.

2   Choose the resources by themes – for example: 'African art', ' modern art', 'landscapes', 'still life' and 'portraits'.

3   Take people to local art exhibitions, places of interest and historic homes. Set aside some time during these visits to ask people what they liked or disliked, and encourage them to explain why.

4   Keep a record (photocopies, prints, photographs, notes) of work chosen by the group, including names of people participating. Return, with the same group, to look at the work again. See if people feel the same way about the work chosen. Discuss any changes of opinion, and why group members may have changed their minds.

Comments

Some people may find it difficult to describe what they see or feel about the items seen. Avoid putting any pressure on an individual to speak out if they choose not to. If someone's experience of art is limited or non-existent, it may be difficult for them to find the appropriate words or means to express themselves. Be prepared to make or find additional communication tools to enable an individual to join in – for example, cards with descriptive words/pictures on them that the person can point to or select.

Aims

* **To enable group members to learn more about artists and the work they do**
* **To stimulate research skills, understanding, and interest in individual artists, and the motivation behind their work**
* **To offer an opportunity for people to choose a favourite/specific artist, and develop an understanding and knowledge about the artist and their work.**

Materials

* **A selection of resources (books, prints, videos) on various artists through the ages. (Include any current local or international artists you know of.)**
* **Egg-timer, or watch with a second hand.**

Method

Select one book about an artist, or an artist that you are familiar with, and talk about this person and their work to the group for a few minutes. Say what you like and/or dislike about the artist and the work, and explain why: talk for no more than three minutes. Ask the group to look through the resources and select an artist for themselves. Invite group members to take it in turns to share their views on the artist chosen, within the agreed time limit of three minutes.

Speechmark  P

Then encourage the group to hold a general debate on why some artists become famous and others do not – especially after they die!

Alternatives

1 Look out for television programmes/videos on individual artists that you can show the group. Focus on one artist only.

2 Ask group members to research and prepare a presentation, lasting three minutes, on a famous artist, or artist of their choice, for the following week.

3 If people are keen, start a scrapbook or resource file on the various artists people have chosen. Include comments about the group members' reactions to the artists' work. This can be done individually or as a group. Talk about the different ways to research and find information on these artists – for example, the local library, the internet, local and national exhibitions and book shops.

4 Visit an exhibition about a specific artist. Discuss group members' likes and dislikes, and how the artists and their works have been portrayed in the exhibitions. How effective was the exhibition in telling others about the artists and their works? How could this have been done differently?

5 Ask group members if they consider themselves to be artists. If 'Yes', then why? If 'No', why not? What aspect of their artwork would they like to be famous for? – for example, their style, techniques, messages in the work, or because it shocks or pleases other people.

6 If group members were suddenly able to paint/draw/work like a famous artist, who would that be, and why? Encourage discussion of these points.

Comments

Consider including work by local artists and art students. Try to include a wider variety of opportunities for exploring a range of artists and art forms. Where possible, involve the group in the research and selection of artists and exhibitions.

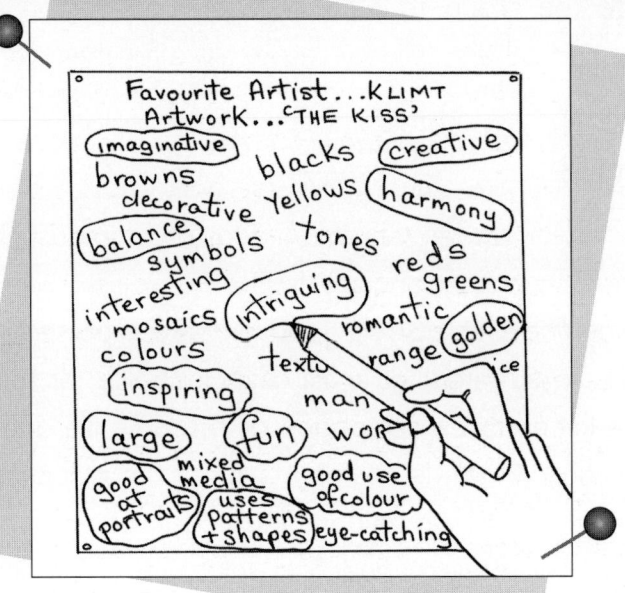

Favourite Artist...KLIMT
Artwork...'THE KISS'
imaginative blacks creative
browns decorative Yellows harmony
balance symbols tones reds greens
interesting intriguing romantic golden
mosaics colours texture range
inspiring man
large fun wor
good at portraits mixed media uses patterns + shapes good use of colour eye-catching

Aims

* **To encourage group members to appraise the world of art critically, and gain knowledge and insight into their own views and feelings about art**

* **To enable people to identify a favourite piece of artwork and its artist, and discover what makes the work successful from their perspective, and why**

* **To offer the opportunity for group members to assess their own artistic aspirations, by becoming aware of their own thoughts on what makes a successful work of art or artist, and considering how this can be applied in their own practice.**

Materials

* **A selection of pictures, prints, books, or postcards of various artworks and their artists – make a random selection that spans time historically and culturally**

* **Large sheets of paper, and various coloured felt-tip pens**

* **Something with which to attach paper to a wall or the board, such as Sellotape® or BluTack®.**

Method

Select your favourite work of art from the resources chosen. Tell the group why this is your favourite piece, and what you think makes it successful. Say what you know of the artist (if unknown, state unknown). On the large sheet of paper, write words that best describe why you like the work and find it successful. Circle the words (with your choice of coloured pen) that say how you would like to be described when you create your own artworks – for example, 'imaginative', 'creative', 'good use of colour', 'intriguing' and 'golden'.

Invite group members to take it in turns to do the same, or ask the group collectively to write reasons why they think a chosen piece of work is successful, on another sheet of paper. Give a coloured pen to each person, and ask them, in turn, to circle the words that describe them now as artists, or the ways in which they would like to be described. (Colour pens are useful when group members want to be identified individually.) Select the main words chosen by the group, and summarise the choices made on what makes a successful work of art on a separate piece of paper. Where individual artists have used their own colour pens, invite them to select the words they have chosen, and transfer these to a separate sheet of paper for their personal record. Encourage them to put their ideas into practice.

Alternative

Individual group members can develop their own personal profiles by building a collection of pictures, photographs, or sketches of a successful piece of work (either their own work or another artist's). They can then make a spontaneous list of words to describe the work, and select aspects that best describe them as they are now, or would like to be in the future.

Comments

This exercise enables people to look for positive and successful outcomes to art, and identify skills and aspirations within themselves. This is also a useful exercise to enable people to recognise their own strengths, or build goals to improve their skills, and achieve the outcomes they choose for themselves.

Exploring Shape and Form

Aims

* **To increase group awareness of shapes and forms found in the world around us**
* **To use visual and tactile experiences to identify shapes and forms, and to explore the use of words and images to describe these experiences**
* **To enable group members to create a work of art inspired by their observations on shape and form.**

Materials

* **Art Resource Box**
* **Large pictures from magazines, books, information leaflets, postcards and posters featuring shape and form – everyday objects, fruit and vegetables, animals, people, landscape features, sculptures, and abstract or unusual images**
* **A collection of objects that can be handled safely, demonstrating a variety of three-dimensional shapes and forms – for example, pebbles, shells, leaves, boxes, ornaments, fruit, plants**
* **Paper, or natural materials on which to place objects**
* **Paper for drawing/painting**
* **Black/coloured card for mounting work.**

A The World Around Us *(cont'd)*

31

Method

Display the selection of work on tables within the workspace used by the group. Spend approximately 20 minutes with the group, looking at pictures and handling the objects collected. Talk about the shapes and forms identified. Compare the differences between the two-dimensional images and the three-dimensional objects. Use simple language, and encourage group members to describe what they see and feel in their own way. Introduce words yourself if assistance is required – for example, 'round', 'square', 'tall' and 'thin'. Ask group members to choose a shape or form to draw or paint, and encourage people to assist each other. Where necessary, someone can draw an outline shape while others colour it in.

Praise and encourage individual interpretations of the shapes and forms identified. Mount the work on an appropriate black or coloured card to display on the walls and screens. (If possible, do this with the group, or when the session is over, with a couple of willing volunteers from the group.) Talk about the completed work and see how many shapes and forms can be identified – and if any new ones have emerged. Enjoy the experience with the group.

Alternatives

1   Place a large sheet of paper on the wall or table, and encourage group members to take it in turns to produce shapes and forms on the shared paper, inspired by the images and objects viewed earlier.
2   Invite group members to cut out shapes and forms that have been drawn by them (or selected from magazines by those not drawing or painting). Build a communal or individual collage with these cuttings.
3   Identify a shape or form, and encourage group members to doodle on/around this to create new shapes and forms. See if anyone can identify any aspects of their environment in these shapes – for example, animals, faces, trees or other familiar objects.

Comments

Select shapes and forms that are easily identified by the group members, and are familiar to them in their everyday lives. More time may be needed to make and mount the pictures by the group. Some people may find the discussion adequate, and may not wish to participate in a practical way. If so, encourage them to observe or assist the others as appropriate.

This page may be photocopied for instructional use only. *The Art Activity Manual* © Marylyn Cropley 2004

Speechmark P

Aims

* To offer group members an opportunity to explore, identify and understand the structure and diversity of shapes
* To enable people to create and use shapes selectively or randomly, and enjoy the experience.

Materials

* Art Resource Box
* A4 white or pastel cards
* Templates of various shapes (plus square, round and triangle shapes)
* Collage material made from paper only (magazines, wrapping paper, or paper with patterns and textures)
* Solid items that can be drawn around to create shapes – for example wooden blocks, tiles, coins, lids, stones, corks and rulers

Method

Spread templates and shapes on a table near the workspace, before the session begins. Place the cards and collage paper nearby. Set out scissors, glue, pencils, and felt-tip pens from the Art Resource Box. When the session begins, select an A4 card and a shape. Demonstrate by drawing around the shape, creating a set of patterns by repeating this process randomly on the card. (Choose other

shapes if desired to vary patterns.) Discuss the outcome of the demonstration with the group. What does the pattern look like? Do people like the shapes repeated, or prefer a single shape on its own? Discuss why. What would they do with the final picture? Add colour? Add textures? Leave it as it is?

Ask group members to select their own templates or solid shapes and have a go themselves. Offer an alternative by inviting people to use the collage paper to create shapes with prints and patterns on them already, and paste these shapes on to the card. Encourage people to follow their instincts when outlines are drawn, to either fill them in with colour, shading, lines, or leave them as they are. Before the session ends, allow time for individuals to share their work if they want to. Encourage them to describe how they felt using the shapes and creating the images. What effect do the shapes have on the final image? Is it pleasing to the eye? Do shapes complement each other or clash? Discuss how they can display or store completed pieces of work.

Alternatives

1 Create shapes in other ways. 'Draw' shapes in the air, on someone's back, or describe a shape verbally, and ask people to try to draw it on paper, or copy the demonstration.

2 Go to the local beach (if you have one!) or use a tray of sand to draw shapes in the sand. Add stones, shells and natural objects for texture.

Comments

Some people may have difficulty drawing around the shapes and using templates, and will need assistance with this. Have some shapes already cut out for people to select and stick on with glue, Velcro® strips or double-sided tape. Use self-adhesive labels to make shapes, or create a magnetic board, using a metal tray and self-adhesive magnetic strips stuck on to the back of shapes. Felt shapes placed on a square sheet of sandpaper or felt can also do the trick. This will enable those with limited dexterity to participate, by choosing shapes and building a picture with little assistance.

Building Images

Aims

* **To create images and artwork using various shapes and forms**
* **To enable group members to gain some understanding of how shapes and forms can affect the composition of a piece of work**
* **To encourage teamwork, and the sharing of ideas.**

Materials

* **Art Resource Box**
* **Templates of various shapes**
* **A variety of pictures/images that give clear outlines of shapes and forms – line drawings and illustrations from children's books are useful**
* **A selection of shapes already cut out from paper or material that can be used to build a collage**
* **Magazines and pictures that can be cut up to create shapes**
* **Large sheet of card (A3) placed on wall, display board, floor or table – whatever suits the group best.**

Method

Show the group the pictures/images you have collected. Encourage them to look closely at the pictures, and identify the shapes and forms that can be seen in these images – for example, the 'round sun', 'rectangular buildings' and 'squiggly trees'. Discuss how they contribute to the final image. (Allow people to use whatever language best describes the shapes – within reason!)

PART II: EXPLORING SHAPE AND FORM

Select an image with the group or describe one together – the local park, a garden, plant-pots, a house, mountains; anything goes! Elect one person or several people, to draw a very simple outline of the chosen image on the A3 card. Do not worry if it is not realistic. Encourage people to look for the shapes and forms, and 'block out' some of the shapes identified on the picture by outlining them with a thick felt-tip pen – for example, the square-shaped house, the tall tree, or a round bush. Ask group members to 'fill in' the picture, by cutting to size and sticking on the collage materials and shapes. A collage can be built by using shapes singly or layered on the A3 picture.

When the picture is complete, discuss the outcome and process with the group. What worked, and what did not? What colours, textures and shapes were chosen, and why? What impact did these have on the picture? Was it pleasing, real, abstract, colourful and fun? What did people learn from this experience?

Alternatives

1 Use three-dimensional shapes and forms to build a group sculpture – stacking boxes and light wooden shapes (totem-pole style), or sticking together cardboard boxes, polystyrene shapes and found objects, all work well.
2 Visit places of interest. Use the natural environment to build pictures and structures – this could be the beach, the local forest, someone's back garden or the local scrap-yard.
3 Go to local exhibitions, garden centres or art and craft shops, to see how shape and form are used in different ways.

Comments

Encourage a fun, supportive atmosphere. Allocate tasks to people and encourage teamwork. One person can cut, while another selects the shapes, and a third sticks them on. Keep the discussion optional, as some people may not want to analyse the work. Try to end the session on a positive note. Depending on group preferences, this activity can be done individually, in pairs or as small groups.

Using a large card placed on a wall allows people to stand back and observe the process and the whole image from a distance. This also enables those who are less mobile to participate. The card can also be placed lower to enable someone in a wheelchair to join in.

Exploring Lines and Patterns

Aims

* **To develop an awareness of lines and patterns in our surroundings**
* **To offer the opportunity to use lines and patterns creatively, and enjoy the process**
* **To enable the production of a piece of artwork using lines and patterns.**

Materials

* **Art Resource Box**
* **A4 paper**
* **Samples of patterns, lines and textures familiar in everyday life**
* **Photographs; pictures of architecture, designs, fashion, patterns in our surroundings; books; natural patterns and work by other artists.**

Method

Study the samples with the group. Look closely at the lines and textures within an image, and the patterns they form. How much of our everyday life incorporates lines and patterns? Look at the ways in which lines and patterns are used by artists in their work. Consider a range of art from medieval to modern, and encourage group discussion.

Invite group members to choose a drawing tool from the Art Resource Box, and to copy some of the lines and patterns from the samples that appealed to them. Ask them to design their own images using lines and patterns. Discuss how these

could be used in their everyday lives – for example to decorate clothing, cakes, wallpaper, wrapping paper, or in a work of art. Encourage group members to start a sketchbook in which to collect a store of patterns and designs that appeal to them, or which may be useful for future artwork. Discuss how the sketchbook could be used regularly, and what format it should take.

Alternatives

1   Take the group out to study the environment in the local community. Look at flowers, trees and plants, both indoors and out. Study fashion in the streets and in shopping areas. Study the local architecture, offices, churches, outsides of shops, old and new structures.
2   Use the written word to create patterns. Explore ancient patterns and languages used by other civilisations, such as the Egyptians and the Romans.
3   Print patterns using print blocks or small objects and poster paints – cork stoppers, sponges, scrunched up paper, and other similarly textured objects work well.

Comments

A good way to store ideas and cuttings on patterns and lines is to file them in clear plastic sleeves. These can be obtained in A5 or A4 sizes. Photocopy and enlarge pictures to get a different image of textures and patterns.

Making Designs

Aims

* **To encourage group members to observe, and share their views on, the ways in which lines and patterns are used in everyday designs**
* **To offer an opportunity to create a personal design, using lines and patterns, that can be used to decorate an item of clothing such as a T-shirt**
* **To gain some awareness of, and insight into, personal tastes, and an appreciation of pattern and design.**

Materials

* **Art Resource Box**
* **Samples of patterns and designs found in everyday life, especially on fashion and household items**
* **A4 paper**
* **White T-shirts of various sizes, purchased new or from charity shops, washed and ironed; or cotton squares, ironed**
* **Fabric paints or crayons**
* **Newspapers**
* **Iron and ironing board, depending on the kind of fabric paints used.**

Method

Look at the samples of patterns and lines with the group. Discuss likes, dislikes, effectiveness, colours, textures, and whether or not the patterns complement the items they decorate. Ask people, individually or in pairs, to create a pattern or design that they would like to see on a T-shirt, either for themselves or someone else. Offer time for discussion if needed. Invite people to select a T-shirt or cotton

This page may be photocopied for instructional use only. The Art Activity Manual © Marylyn Cropley 2004

square to draw on. Suggest that they experiment with sketches on paper or a sketchbook, before choosing the pattern they want to use. Offer some time for the group to make their sketches. When they have finished, suggest that they can transfer their pattern on to a chosen material or T-shirt, by using a pencil first, or painting directly on to the fabric with the fabric paints if they are feeling bold!

Show group members how to do this, by choosing some material, and placing it on top of a wad of newspaper. Tape down the material with masking tape if required. Draw some patterns and shapes on the material, randomly or selectively. Ensure that you follow instructions that come with the fabric paint you have chosen. When you have completed your demonstration, encourage group members to have a go. When everyone has finished, discuss the outcome. Were people happy with their designs? Why? What would they change or keep? Where else could the same patterns be used? – possibilities might include cushion covers, curtains, or wrapping paper. If feasible, and all group members are willing, hold a mini fashion parade, with everyone wearing their T-shirts. Suggest that people may want to display their work on walls at home or in a more public place, but emphasise that this is optional.

Alternatives

1 Encourage group members to create designs for other items, such as cushion covers, wrapping paper, scarves, bookmarks and other household items.
2 Offer group members an opportunity to decorate ceramic plates, plant-pots or even wellington boots with acrylic paints.
3 Hold sessions that focus on encouraging and enabling group members to keep a scrapbook of their favourite designs. Collect designs from other countries, religions, artists and architecture with the group, to inspire future work. Develop a scrapbook yourself to inspire any future groups you may facilitate.

Comments

Use acrylic paints instead of fabric paints. Note that these dry quickly, and group members may wish to experiment on sample cloths before painting the final T-shirt. Use permanent marker pens instead of fabric crayons. Wear protective clothing, and have additional help if needed!

Doodling

Aims

* To enjoy the process of 'doodling', using lines and patterns either individually or as a group activity
* To be creative, and use the imagination through the process of doodling.

Materials

* Art Resource Box
* A4 or A3 paper
* Tables placed together, and chairs round the table to enable group members to sit in a circle
* A collection of music on tapes/CDs, and a tape/CD player. Have a selection of music offering a wide range of styles and moods – for example, jazz, classical, reggae, instrumental, pop, slow and peaceful, or rhythmical. (Music is optional: some people may prefer to chat, or work in a quieter way).

Method

Place the tables together, and seat the group around the table to enable work to be passed from person to person. Place a variety of drawing/colouring media in the centre of the table – for example pencils, crayons, pastels, charcoal and felt-tip pens. Give each person in the group a sheet of paper, and ask them to put

This page may be photocopied for instructional use only. The Art Activity Manual © Marilyn Cropley 2004

their name on the back. Select a piece of relaxation music to begin with, and play this to the group. Ask individuals to turn their paper over, start the music (softly), and invite people to draw lines and patterns on the paper in front of them. Encourage them to do this spontaneously and randomly, and not worry about the outcome.

Stop the music at regular intervals (after a minute or two), and ask people to pass their sheet to the person on their right. Start the music again, and encourage people to doodle on the next sheet of paper in front of them, continuing until everyone has their original sheet back (hence the names on the reverse). Ask people if they wish to change or add any lines to the work in front of them. Explain that this is not compulsory. When all is finished, observe the completed pieces of work, and encourage group discussion. Ask what people think of the final work: did they mind sharing their doodle with others? How do the lines and patterns appear? Were they compatible, random or consistent?

Discuss ways to display or use the work – for example in a book, on the wall, as a montage, or cut into smaller pieces to use for collage. Group members could try doodling on the patterns all over again to see what happens. If there is time, ask a group member to select another piece of music, and offer an opportunity to do the exercise again. Some may wish to have another go, while others may just want to listen to the music until the end of the session.

Alternatives

1   Create random doodles by using print blocks, paints and other media.
2   Cut up and glue on paper shapes, or self-adhesive dots and shapes. Use these randomly, or to create consistent patterns and designs.
3   Splash paint or ink randomly on to wet, absorbent paper or blotting paper. See what shapes emerge, and doodle outlines and patterns inspired by these shapes.

Comments

For those with limited manual dexterity, place your hand over their hand, and have fun doodling randomly. Use other methods to make patterns, such as trailing a piece of string, which has been dipped in paint, over the paper. Hold long feathers or twigs, and run them over the paper to see what happens. Use long-handled paintbrushes, and make sure there is sufficient space around each person for larger movements. Be non-judgemental, and enjoy the process.

42

Exploring Textures

Aims

* **To identify and define what is meant by 'texture'**
* **To understand how texture is used in art, and in our environment**
* **To experience and describe texture, from visual and tactile perspectives.**

Materials

* **A selection of materials and objects that demonstrate textures in various ways, and are safe to handle – for example, pebbles, sandpaper, silk/cotton, scarves, wool, string, fur, wax candles, woven mats, painted surfaces and collage**
* **Photographs and pictures showing objects, landscapes, and images that demonstrate artificial and natural textures – for example, flowers, leaves, tree trunks, brick/stone walls, a collection of pebbles on sand, grass and sheep.**

Method

Offer round the selection of materials and objects for the group to touch and observe. Encourage participants to call out words spontaneously, to describe to the group how the items feel or look. Encourage people to assist each other, and prompt if necessary. Ask the group to create a definition of 'texture'. What does it mean to them? If necessary, give your own definition, or quote from the dictionary. Discuss the impact of texture on a work of art, or in the environment. What would life be like without texture? What effect does 'texture' have on people, when touched or seen? What are the likes/dislikes of group members concerning texture? If possible, encourage them to explain their preferences.

Alternative

Create 'touch cards'. Cut out several square cards, and stick various 'textures' on to the cards – for example, thick/thin paint, collage, pieces of scouring pad, sandpaper, cotton wool, string, dried beans, lace, buttons, and natural objects. Watch out for sharp corners and edges!

Comments

This exercise may be difficult for some people, for various reasons, physical or emotional. Be aware of this, and be prepared to offer additional support if needed. Be sensitive, and emphasise that touching the items is optional. If someone does not want to touch something immediately, leave the item nearby, and allow the person to have control as to when to touch, if at all. Participation can still be accomplished by observation, and by joining in with conversations.

Some members of the group may prefer to start by touching something they are wearing or own, such as the sleeve of their jumper, their skirt, their hair, or the back of a hand, and describe how this feels. Alternatively, observe what the person already touches in their immediate environment – for example, the table, an arm of a chair/wheelchair, a book, or the person next to them. Feeling confident in handling art materials and having some control over this is important, particularly when trying to enable people to enjoy art, and the variety of tactile media that is on offer.

B Creating Textures

Aims

* **To offer group members the opportunity to use a variety of techniques and media to create textures**
* **To use the textures created to produce a communal work of art, a textured wall.**

Materials

* **Art Resource Box**
* **A ceramic wall tile**
* **Several sheets of thick card or mount board**
* **A variety of textured materials/fabric to stick on to the card**
* **Samples of textured squares.**

Method

Prior to the session, prepare three or four samples of textured squares. Do this by using a ceramic tile as a template. Place the tile on a piece of thick card, and draw around it. Cut out squares from the card, and glue various textured fabrics on to them – for example, felt, silk, cotton, or net, and materials such as sandpaper, cotton wool and string. Also make as many blank square cards as possible from the template before the session begins, for the group to use. At the start of the session, show the sample cards and blank tiles to the group, and explain that this will be a shared exercise to create a textured wall.

Ask group members to split into pairs or small groups. Allocate tasks, or encourage people to choose a task, to enable the group to build a textured wall collectively with the cards. Some will need to make the textured squares with

This page may be photocopied for instructional use only. *The Art Activity Manual* © Marylyn Cropley 2004

the square cards, materials and fabrics, while others start to build the 'wall'. When the tiles are completed and dry, ask people to attach double-sided tape or Velcro® strips on the back, at all four corners. They can use this to attach the tile to a wall, or another larger mount, in rows, to create a montage/wall effect. Discuss and evaluate the finished work. Encourage people to touch the tiles, and compare textures.

Alternative

Collect cardboard boxes from the local supermarket (or other such source), choosing boxes that will stack to give a totem-pole structure. Glue the lids down, and paint the boxes white. Stack and glue boxes together for stability. Stick the textured tiles around the sides of the boxes, in rows or formats chosen by the group. This type of structure can be moved around or stacked in a variety of ways – experiment!

Comments

If you are unable to use a wall to build a montage, try to borrow free-standing display boards. Encourage the group to touch the tiles, and enjoy the process of building a textured wall together.

Tactile Pictures

Aims

✳ **To construct pictures that are tactile as well as visual**

✳ **To explore the differences between tactile and non-tactile images, and the impression this has on individual group members.**

Materials

✳ **Art Resource Box**
✳ **Images of simple line drawings, shapes, and landscapes – some children's books are good sources of simple illustrations**
✳ **A4 paper and cards**
✳ **Cut-up pieces of paper and textured materials**
✳ **Tracing paper/grease-proof paper.**

Method

Lay out the tracing paper and other materials on a table, near to where the group will be seated. Show the resources to the group, and, if needed, demonstrate how to use the tracing paper. Then, as a group, look at the simple illustrations or line drawings more closely. Ask people to select a scene or image that they want to copy. Encourage people to trace or copy the basic outline shapes of these images on to the A4 paper, using the tracing paper provided, or by copying freehand. Ask people to make two copies of the same image, or use a photocopier if possible.

Suggest that each person then colour or shade in one of the pictures with pencils or crayons to produce a fairly smooth surface. They can then fill in the shapes of the second copy with the materials and paper already cut up, to create a collage with a textured surface. Observe and discuss the differences between the pictures with the smooth, coloured-in surface, and those with the collage, textured surface. Explore the colours, shapes and textures used in the pictures, and the effect this has on the overall image.

Alternatives

1 Encourage people to create their own images using textured materials. Create random, abstract shapes and textures, without the need to draw first. Fill in images with thick PVA glue, and add texture by sprinkling sand, salt or small, dried pulses/beans on to the glue. Use tissue paper, scrunched paper, kitchen rolls and similar materials to create textures.

2 Make lined, textured 'drawings' with string or glue. Pencil in lines as a guide, or create images randomly. Use the string to outline shapes, glue it on with PVA glue, and paint over or cover it with layers of tissue paper when dry. Draw with the PVA glue, using a glue bottle with a nozzle top. Place the nozzle of the glue bottle at the start of the image, squeeze gently and follow the line drawing with the glue, or doodle randomly. When the end is reached, lift the bottle quickly to avoid drips. Leave the work to dry overnight, and paint over with acrylics or poster paints.

Comments

To make it easier and save time, you can photocopy a simple picture twice over in black and white, once on paper and then on card. Ask group members to colour or shade in the paper version, and add textures to the card version, to enable a comparison of textures.

Exploring Light and Dark

Aims

* To gain an understanding of tonal values used in art, beginning with black and white
* To create images boldly and with confidence, using black and white
* To experiment with, and understand, the ways in which light and shadow can affect an image.

Materials

* Art Resource Box
* Pictures of landscapes, people, objects and animals, in colour and in black and white. (Photocopy the colour images in black and white also.)
* Photocopies of a selection of black and white photographs that show strong contrasts and tones.

Method

Begin with a general discussion on the effect of light and shadow in our environment and everyday lives. Explain to the group that the purpose of this exercise is to explore the extremes of light and dark, by using black and white images only. Demonstrate first to the group by selecting a black and white photocopy of an image. Using soft pencils, graphite or charcoal, shade over the darker areas till they are as black as possible. Decide which areas to leave white. If possible, identify where the light may be coming from, and what impact this has

This page may be photocopied for instructional use only. The Art Activity Manual © Marylyn Cropley 2004

Speechmark P

on the final picture. Invite people to select a black and white image and do the same. Discuss the final outcome, and, where there is an identical colour picture, compare it with the black and white version. What is the difference between the black and white and colour images? Is one better than the other? Why? Do people have a preference?

Alternatives

1   Use white chalk on black card. Experiment with different media, such as paint and collage. Stick white shapes on to black backgrounds, and vice versa.
2   Place a still life on the table in middle of the room, and encourage people to draw it, using black and white only. For special effects, shine a bright light on the still life to create light and shadows.

Comments

Encourage people to be bold! Make the black as black, and the white as white, as possible. Look to the environment for ideas and inspiration. Study the use of black and white in fashion, designs in furniture and work by other artists, both in the past and in the present.

B Shades of Grey

Shades of Grey

Aims

* **To experiment with tones, by mixing black and white**
* **To create images by mixing black and white, and experimenting with shades of grey.**

Materials

* **Art Resource Box**
* **Paper**
* **Pictures that demonstrate various 'shades of grey' – for example, photographs, books from the library, cuttings from magazines, and pictures of work by other artists.**

Method

Study the pictures with the group, and discuss the effect of having just grey in images and in the environment. How many shades of grey can people identify in the images? Inform the group that they will be making a grid of squares depicting different shades of grey, using rulers and black and white paint from the Art Resource Box. (They can do this individually or collectively.)

They will need to draw the squares first to make a grid of any size the group chooses, and may need assistance to do this if the grid is to be large. Suggest that they make large squares if using paints, and smaller ones, if using pencils or chalks to shade in. If in doubt, encourage people to begin with large squares, using paint – poster paints will do. It may be helpful to suggest that people start at the top left-hand corner of the grid, making this square as black as possible, by using the black paint on its own. Then they can gradually add a little white paint to the black, and paint in the next square. They need to repeat this process so that each square gradually lightens in shade until the final square is white. The whole grid should display a gradual progression from black, through shades of grey, to white.

When the grid is finished, and if time allows, ask group members to then draw their own pictures, abstract or real. Encourage them to paint these in, using only shades of grey. They can try mixing the paints separately in containers, or build up the shades by painting straight onto the picture, and adding black to certain parts. Suggest they try painting white on top when the black dries out or is still wet. Encourage people to experiment with images, in which black and white blend or contrast in a random fashion. Enjoy the process. Discuss the finished work. How does it look? Do people like the effect of grey images? Do they feel they need to add colour? Why?

Alternatives

1   Encourage group members to create black and white sketchbooks. Ask people to collect images, make sketches using soft pencils, and shade in their work in various greys.

2   Where possible, go out and about with the group on a bright sunny day, to observe how the light can create shadows when it shines on natural objects, statues, buildings and people. Observe how the shadows move, growing longer, or shorter, depending on where the light is coming from. Is everything black and white, or shades of grey? Can they see grey in the colours they notice? Go into woods, caves (if possible), or out at night with a strong torch, and observe the effect of light on dark, and the differences between very black and very white, and what lies in between. Discuss and explore, encouraging people to be observant whenever possible.

Comments

Encourage people to use black and white chalks, or charcoal sticks on a white background in sessions, as this gives lots of scope to smudge, blend and experiment with shades and tones. Also make use of collage materials, such as newspapers, textiles, black and white photographs (photocopied), or images from magazines.

Aims

* To have some understanding of how white, black or grey can affect tonal qualities when mixed with colour
* To use primary colours (red, yellow and blue) with combinations of white, black or grey to create a communal abstract picture – a tonal mural.

Materials

* Art Resource Box
* A3 paper or a large roll
* Paintings by artists that demonstrate use of colour, and variations in the brightness and darkness of the colours
* Books showing the colour wheel, and demonstrating use of colour.

Method

Begin by looking at the pictures, and talking about the colours found in the images. Are the colours bright, dark or in-between? Are they very light or very dark? Ask group members to find the darkest colours and the brightest colours. Explain how light and dark (or black and white), can affect the tone of the colour, and discuss the ways in which the tone of one colour can affect the colour next to it – for example, yellow will stand out brighter next to a darker tone of blue or red.

Encourage everyone to look at the books showing the colour wheel. Talk about the primary and secondary colours, and how they affect each other when placed side by side or mixed together. Discuss how using white, black or grey with

This page may be photocopied for instructional use only. The Art Activity Manual © Marylyn Cropley 2004

colours may affect the tone of the colour, making it brighter, darker or 'muddy'. Now experiment! Set out containers of paint (poster paints, or media chosen by group), with primary colours (red, yellow and blue). Have a selection of black, white and grey paints also. Ask people to experiment with mixing colours, to make colours as dark or as bright as they can. Encourage people to find other tones by mixing the colours with a little white, black or grey.

Place a large sheet of paper on the wall, a display board, or the floor. Cut or tear abstract shapes from the work done by the group, and invite group members to build an abstract tonal mural by gluing these shapes on to the large sheet of paper. Encourage people to observe and consider where they place the shapes, and how the colours and tones affect each other when placed side by side. If using paint, you may need to allow time for the paint to dry first.

Alternatives

1 Create tonal murals, using only one colour. Split the group into three smaller groups, if possible, and ask one group to make a red mural, using only shades of red mixed with black, white and greys. Have the next group paint a blue mural next to the red, and the third group create a yellow one. Ask people to try to identify the very bright tones from the dark within each colour, and see if there is a difference. This is a good exercise in enabling people to identify colours, and to demonstrate that different tones can be found within the same colour.

2 Use still life to enable group members to observe colour and tone. Place objects in a bright light, and encourage people to observe the colour and tones of the objects, which might include flowers, a bowl of fruit, brightly coloured scarves crumpled in a heap, bright paper scrunched up, or bright ornaments and vases with simple shapes.

Comments

Modern art is a good source of inspiration when working with colour and tone. Enable the group to look at modern paintings and abstract art, and to have a go at copying the images and colours. Reassure people that their picture does not have to be an exact copy: the process itself is a good learning experience. Enjoy the outcome, and talk about what was gained from the experience.

A 'What is Colour?'

Exploring Colour

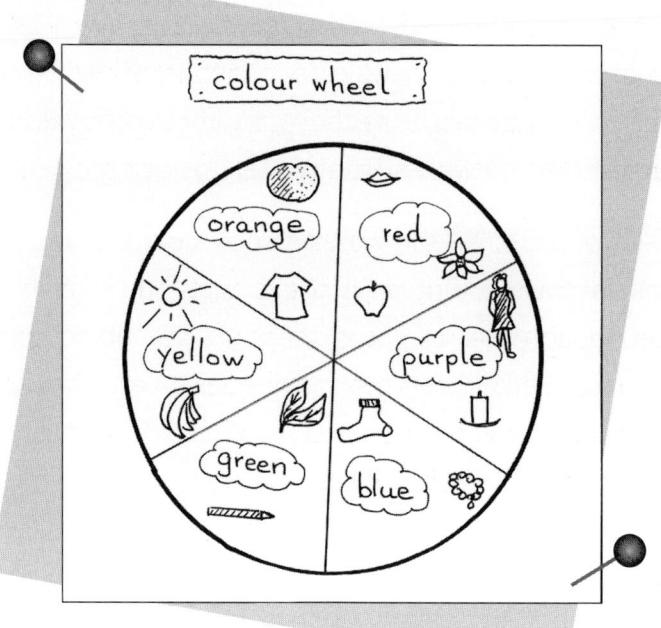

Aims

* To build an awareness of colour in everyday life and the environment we live in
* To gain a general understanding of how individuals perceive colour
* To create a large 'colour wheel', as a group project.

Materials

* Art Resource Box
* Large sheets of paper/card
* Magazines/pictures with coloured shapes and images to cut up
* Books/photographs that show the use of colour, in fashion design and art
* Books that give a simple explanation (with colour diagrams) of the 'colour wheel'.

Method

Begin with a general discussion on colour. Ask people to identify colours they see in their immediate environment – for example, the clothes they are wearing, objects in the room, walls, furniture, and what they see through the window. Encourage people to describe the colours they like/dislike, and ask them to explain their preferences. Using the art books, display an image of the 'colour wheel' and talk about the primary and secondary colours. Explain that you are going to build a large 'colour wheel' together.

Draw a large circle on paper or card, and divide this into six sections (as in the picture on page 54). Use one section for each of the primary and secondary colours initially, to keep it simple – only include tertiary colours at this point if this seems useful to the group, and is not confusing. It may be easier to cut out the sections, and split the group into pairs when painting each section. Have two people paint each section with a colour from the wheel, until the group has built the complete wheel. Place the whole colour wheel on a wall, display board or floor.

Have some group members cut out images from the magazines showing the primary and secondary colours. Paste these on to the appropriate colour sections of the colour wheel – for example, place a lady wearing a red dress on the red section of wheel. When the wheel is complete, encourage members to discuss the pictures they have chosen. Do the colours differ? Notice the various shades of colour, and how the value and intensity of the colours match, or do not match, those on the colour wheel. (Some blues may be lighter or darker than other blues, for example.) Ask people to identify the colours they like/dislike, and to explain their choices. Has this changed from the start of the session?

Alternatives

1 Build a sturdy and more permanent colour wheel from cardboard or wood, so that it can be used many times. Use BluTack® or Velcro® pads to stick items on to the colour wheel, so that they can be changed from time to time.

2 Look through magazines and books with the group, noticing how colour is used to advertise products and influence people. Ask them to see if the colours used complement each other, and, in the case of fashion pictures, if they complement the model wearing the colours. Do the clothes they wear go with the colour of their hair, eyes, or the accessories they are wearing?

3 Take the group for a walk and encourage group members to look at the colours used on cars, buildings, advertisements and the clothes people wear. Then compare these colours to the natural colours found in trees, plants, sky and animals. This is a good exercise to enable people to remember colours, and appreciate its diversity in our environment.

Comments

Be aware that some people may be colour-blind. Help them to compare with others the colours they see, and clarify colours they are not sure of. Reassure them that this should not stop them enjoying and using colour: there are many good artists who create the most amazing, colourful images, but who are colour-blind!

Aims

* **To create images, using colours and media chosen by individual group members**
* **To have the opportunity to experiment freely with colour, and enjoy the process.**

Materials

* **Art Resource Box**
* **Paper – offer a mixture of papers of different textures, sizes, thicknesses and colours**
* **Books, calendars, postcards and photographs with colourful images to inspire the group – choose a variety of topics, such as animals, plants, people, landscapes and abstract art**
* **Books on different artists (old and new), with colour images of their work, showing the variety of colours and media used by each artist.**

Method

Spread out a variety of art materials from the Art Resource Box on a table – use pastels, crayons, oils, acrylics, watercolours, pencils and chalks. Also spread out the paper, to enable people to have a choice. Explain that this is a free session, during which people can paint or draw any picture or image they choose, real or imaginary, using paper and media of their own choosing. Some people will know

what they want to do and will start straight away; others will panic! Be supportive, and look through the books and images with them. Ask individuals to select an image that appeals to them.

Encourage people to try to copy the images and colours chosen. Emphasise that it does not have to be an exact copy. If feeling brave, suggest they try something from their imagination. If someone is struggling for a subject matter, help them to choose a topic or word at random – for example, 'a day by the sea', 'frogs' or 'trees'. Suggest that group members compare their completed work with the original picture or idea, but do this in a positive, non-judgemental way.

Encourage group members to try the same image with different paper and media. Why did they choose the colours and materials they did? What did they enjoy and learn from the experience? Which paper or medium did they prefer to use, and why?

Alternatives

1   If preferred, encourage people to doodle with colour, selecting colours and creating abstract shapes and lines freely. They may see other images in the finished work, and go on to create a picture from this.

2   Ask people to allow colours to dry, and then layer colour upon colour. Mix a little paint with PVA glue/water and create a glaze effect when layering colours.

3   Encourage people to have a go at spraying water on or wetting their paper with a brush first, then painting 'wet' on 'wet', observing the effect this has on the colours used.

4   Suggest that people use the same image several times, using one colour only each time – for example, they can photocopy a landscape or simple line drawing several times in black and white, then paint each copy in a different, single colour. They can also use different shades of colour in the paintings, if desired. People can trace over images if they find it difficult to copy freehand. They can then block in the images traced, using a colour similar to the original, or try different colours. Invite people to be outrageous with the colours they use. Compare pictures, and select the preferred piece.

Comments

Some people may feel nervous about working in this way, especially if new to groups or using colour. They may prefer to observe others to begin with. To help break the ice, invite them to do a joint picture with you, or someone they are comfortable with in the group.

Colour and Expression

Aims

* To have some understanding, and explore the use, of colour in expressing ideas, feelings, thoughts and images in art.

Materials

* A selection of colourful images/shapes from books, magazines, photographs, calendars, or three-dimensional objects, showing art and colour from different periods and cultures
* A collection of soft scarves/materials, each showing one colour only. Collect as wide a variety of colours as possible – charity shops and car boot sales are good places to look!
* Colour samples/brochures from DIY and carpet/furniture stores, showing a wide range of colours.

Method

Begin with a general discussion on colour and expression. Ask group members to look through the images collected, and identify how colours are used to express ideas or feelings. Invite people to share their views on specific colours, their likes/dislikes, and how certain colours make them feel. Talk about how colours can

This page may be photocopied for instructional use only. *The Art Activity Manual* © Marylyn Cropley 2004

PART II: EXPLORING COLOUR

affect emotions, feelings and even memories. Mention cultural and religious differences in colour usage, and the way these may alter our perception of colour.

Place the coloured scarves/materials in the centre of the group. Ask each person to choose a scarf and hold it for a moment. Recommend that each person concentrates on the colour chosen, and tries to 'see' that colour with their eyes closed. If they want to, they could describe how the colour made them feel. Invite people to think about a feeling, object, or idea, and find a colour that best describes it – for example, yellow for 'happiness', 'custard', 'banana', and 'sunshine', or green for 'jealousy', 'apple', 'calmness' or 'nature'.

Display the colour sample, and ask people to think about a room in their house, encouraging them to select the colours they would choose to decorate this room. Discuss why they chose those colours for that specific room. Alternatively, think about a special occasion (wedding, party, holiday), and select colours that people would wear for these occasions. Discuss the group's choices. Some people may not have had much choice in this area of their lives or have given it much thought, so may need encouragement and support to do this.

Alternatives

1 Use themes or short poems/quotations to inspire the use of colour in sessions. Ask people to describe an animal or a person they know, in colour – for example, a grey hippo, or a bright yellow Sally! This can be as realistic or as abstract as they wish.

2 Move away from personal colour preferences, and build a communal colour sketchbook with people in the group. Ask people to collect as many samples of colour as possible, with comments/notes they have made relating to the colours found. Store these in file or sketchbook formats.

3 As a group, create a three-dimensional display or sculpture of objects found by the group, depicting different colours, liked or disliked. Encourage discussion about the work.

Comments

Sometimes, when relating colour to feelings, people may be reminded about experiences that could make them emotional. It is important to acknowledge this, validate the person's response, and to reassure them that this happens. Make supportive contingency plans and try to end the session on a positive, humorous and colourful note.

'What Makes a Picture?'

Composition and Perspective

Aims

* **To enable group members to explore and evaluate the effect of using composition and perspective in artwork.**

Materials

* **Books on perspective – information books designed for children give simple explanations**
* **Art books demonstrating use of perspective/composition through the ages – for example, primitive, Egyptian, Roman, Chinese, Byzantine, medieval, contemporary, modern art and cubism.**

Method

Begin by having a general group discussion on what is meant by 'perspective'. In everyday life, how do people perceive the space and objects around them? When do things seem far away or close? How do we know whether something is round or flat? How do we know whether something is moving or standing still? Encourage people to look through the art books, and discuss how the artists interpret what they see in their work. How do they interpret three-dimensional

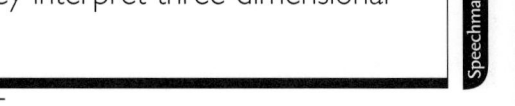

objects and spaces on flat surfaces? Does everything look real/unreal, and why? How do they make things look far away and near by?

Point out the flat images in medieval and Egyptian art, and ask people to compare these with Roman and contemporary art, with depictions of landscape and views that give a sense of perspective. What are the differences? Discuss the composition of pictures. Where are things placed? Do they look balanced? If not, why not? What would people keep/change in the picture, and why? Encourage members to give honest opinions about what they see, in a non-judgemental atmosphere.

Alternative

Offer the opportunity for group members to look into a mirror, and to describe what they see. Encourage people to look past their own image, and again, to describe what they see. Do objects look flat or three-dimensional? How can they tell? Are things near or far? Do they look different when seen in a mirror? Some people do not like looking at themselves in a mirror, especially in public! If so, ask them to hold the mirror to one side so it reflects the space behind them and not their face. Use the mirror outside in open spaces, and view different scenes. Discuss and share findings.

Comments

Where possible, find out as much as you can about the artists, and the reasoning behind their work, especially where this raises controversy and a high level of interest within the group. Use this information to further challenge and stimulate the group, from a more informed basis. Some artists deliberately 'play' with perspective, to create a sense of illusion, or to challenge and shock. Some may have realised that they were most skilled in abstract or surreal styles, rather than in interpreting perspectives realistically.

It is important to explain that many artists created perspective, and developed their compositions, through trial and error. If people want to learn a more technical/scientific approach to this (such as the 'vanishing point', and the 'golden section'), encourage them to look up this information in art books, or join local art classes to further develop their knowledge/skills.

PART II: COMPOSITION AND PERSPECTIVE 8

Composing a Picture

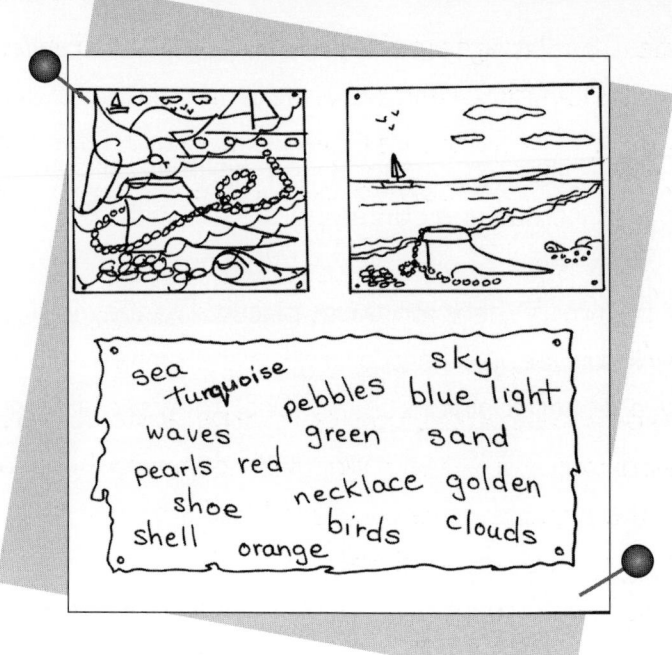

Aims

* **To enable group members to gain an understanding of composition and perspective, while creating a picture together.**

Materials

* **Art Resource Box**
* **Large sheet of paper/card**
* **Three interesting items – for example, a pebble, a necklace and an odd shoe.**

Method

Explain to the group that they are going to create a scene together. The scene can be anything, but must have the three chosen items in it – for example, a pebble, a necklace and an odd shoe. Ask the group to call out any words that spring to mind when they observe these items. Write these words yourself on a large sheet of paper, placed where everyone can see it. Invite the group to create a scene inspired by the words called out – for example, looking out to sea from a pebble beach, with the necklace and shoe abandoned on the beach. Ask for volunteers to draw this scene on another large sheet of paper. This can be done by one member of the group, or by all the volunteers taking turns.

Encourage discussion as to where things will go in the picture, and have the volunteers draw this on the paper as people decide. Will there be a horizon? Will things disappear in the distance? Will there be a boat or two? Seagulls? Far or near? Will the shoe be the largest item in the picture, and where should it be? How large will the pebbles be, and how many? Where do they want to place the

This page may be photocopied for instructional use only. *The Art Activity Manual* © Marilyn Cropley 2004

PART II: COMPOSITION AND PERSPECTIVE

Speechmark

necklace? Do they make images look three-dimensional or flat? How do they do this? Do they add colour, or leave the picture as it is? What colours can they use, and where will the light and dark areas be? Let the group take the lead, and stop when they choose to. Talk about the experience, and what they learnt while composing the scene.

Alternatives

1 Have a session where the group can create abstract pictures using only colours, lines, patterns or random words. When finished, encourage people to discuss how the pictures were composed, and whether the final image is flat in perspective, or three-dimensional.

2 If it is a fine day, take some objects outdoors, and place them against a natural background of fields, countryside, the sea, a garden or trees. Place the item on a large rock, log or small stool, and have group members sit on a mat to draw the object, with the chosen scene behind it. Use a square, rectangle or round 'frame' (a picture finder), held at arm's length, to view the scene and select the contents and boundaries for the composition.

3 Look at photographs and postcards together, and discuss the ways in which the pictures are 'framed' and composed. Does it work? What catches the eye first, and why?

Comments

There are other useful 'props' that a facilitator can use for this exercise, such as lists of words, a short poem or extract from a story describing a scene, a newspaper article and photographs.

Near and Far

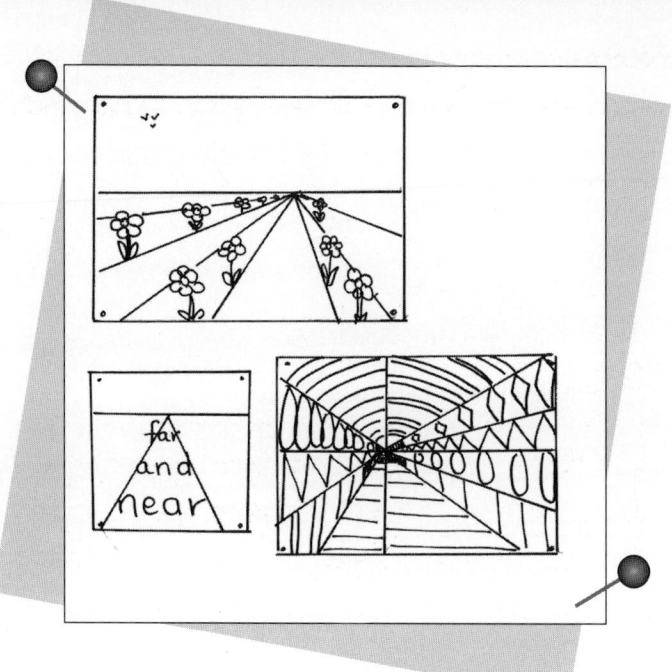

Aims

* **To explore perspective in art, by using the concepts of 'near' and 'far'**
* **To use small and large images to create a picture that gives a sense of 'distance' and 'closeness'.**

Materials

* **Art Resource Box**
* **Large sheet of card or thick paper**
* **Magazines from which to cut out images**
* **Simple images – for example, a sunflower – each image photocopied several times in a range of sizes, from large to small.**
* **Art books demonstrating collage work and perspective**
* **Pictures and photographs, showing views and objects 'near' and 'far', that give a sense of perspective.**

Method

Ask the group to look at the pictures in the books, and the photographs on collage and perspective. Have a general discussion, while looking at the books, on how things appear when further back or nearer to the front of the pictures.

Suggest that group members look at the size of the images, and the lightness/ darkness of the colours in the images. Do the objects appear to recede or come forward? Why?

Next, invite them to create a picture using the photocopied images – for example, use several cut-out images of a flower, ranging from large to small. Using a pencil, draw a straight line half way down the sheet to create a horizon. Place a dot on this horizon, and draw a straight, diagonal line from this dot to the bottom of the sheet of paper at any angle. Place the smallest flower on the dot, and the next largest flower in front of the smallest flower along the diagonal line. Continue, until there is a line of flowers ranging from the largest flower in the front of the picture to the smallest on the horizon. Do not stick the flowers down with glue at this stage (use BluTack® or similar), as they will need to be moved around.

Draw other diagonal lines starting from the dot (or 'vanishing point'), and ending at the bottom edge of the paper. Invite volunteers to come up and move the flowers around the paper, placing them on the lines at different points, while always having the largest flower in front and the smallest towards the vanishing point. Decide together on the best composition, and ask people to glue the flowers on to the paper. Suggest that the group may wish to add other things cut from magazines to the picture, such as trees, bushes, birds, clouds or people. Discuss how big or small these need to be, when placed next to the flowers. Experiment with different images photocopied in the same way, or cut random images from magazines and create a collage, placing smaller images nearer the vanishing point, and larger images towards the front of the picture.

Alternatives

1 Encourage group members to practise the 'vanishing point' concept by drawing a straight line (horizon) across the paper. They then identify a 'vanishing point' on this line with a dot. Next, they draw straight, diagonal lines outwards, each one starting at the dot, creating a network of triangular spaces spreading out from the vanishing point. Now invite them to fill in these spaces with repeated patterns and lines, using vertical lines, circles, rectangles, squares and triangles. They can observe how the shapes recede and become smaller as they approach the vanishing point. They can shade in the patterns with black and white or colours, and experiment with the tones. Encourage them to use either light or dark shades nearer the vanishing point. Ask them to

decide which option gives a sense of distance, or brings shapes forward. Which colours recede or spring forward? Can the tones be described as 'warm' or 'cool'?

2 Go for a walk with the group, and encourage people to look around them to see if the vanishing point can be found on the horizon, looking over fields or at the end of a street.

Comments

Grasping the concept of perspective and composition can be very difficult for anyone striving to be an artist! It is perhaps best to say there are no hard and fast rules to begin with, and to enable people to express themselves freely. Allow and encourage the group to challenge concepts and develop their own interpretations of composition and perspective, in a non-constraining and non-threatening environment. This approach can make a session feel very liberating and exciting, not only for the artists involved, but also for the facilitator.

Exploring Mixed Media

Aims

✳ **To give people the opportunity to explore the contents of the Art Resource Box and experiment with a variety of media and art materials.**

Materials

✳ **Art Resource Box**
✳ **A4 card/thick paper**
✳ **Simple images in black and white, to trace or photocopy.**

Method

Spread out some of the contents from the Art Resource Box – for example, different paints, pastels, various crayons and pencils and a mixture of tools and paper. Explain to the group that this is an opportunity for them to try out the mixed media kept in the Art Resource Box, and to have fun experimenting with these materials to identify what they like to use. This exercise can be done individually, in pairs, or as a group.

Ask group members to select an image, and decide if they want to trace, photocopy or draw the image freehand. Suggest that people select two or three items from the Art Resource Box to begin with (such as charcoal, pastels and pencil) and encourage them to use these items to colour in or decorate the picture chosen, as spontaneously as possible. For example, someone could draw a simple landscape with trees and hills, using pencil or charcoal sticks, then paint a background wash over the landscape with watercolours. They can then add trees and other details using watercolour pencils or oil pastels.

Suggest that people have a go at drawing images with wax crayons, and then paint thin washes over the work with diluted acrylic paint or watercolours. They could also use white chalk to highlight some areas, and graphite pencils to darken others. Encourage people to experiment, have fun, and share ideas and suggestions. When finished, evaluate the work people have done. Ask people which media they enjoyed working with, and why. Think about the subject-matter of each piece: which media best portrayed the subject or the style of the work? What would people do differently next time, and why?

Discuss how to present the work. Ask individuals to choose the work they want to display, keep or dispose of. If possible, keep some work that people would not mind cutting up, to use for collage at another time. Create a display book for future use, and ask people to keep a record of preferences and media chosen.

Alternatives

1 Encourage people to use a variety of tools (as well as a variety of media), such as paintbrushes, sticks, twigs, sponges, cloths, and their fingers. See which tools go well with which media. Add water to the media, or use them dry: how does this make a difference? Introduce other materials to use with those found in the Art Resource Box. For example, sprinkle sand, or crushed, dried leaves, on thick, wet acrylic paint, or sprinkle salt crystals on to wet paint, then shake off when dry. Use unwanted make-up to create weird and wonderful faces.

2 Introduce natural materials to the group, such as burnt wood instead of charcoal, and suggest rubbing grass or flowers on to the paper for stained effects and pleasant tones. 'Paint' with cold tea, coffee or black-currant/carrot juice. Use inks, fabric paints, acrylic and permanent marker pens on scraps of material or blotting paper, instead of the usual paper.

Comments

Exercise caution when using make-up and new materials, especially when working with artists who like to put things in their mouths! Some cosmetics and media are also difficult to get off clothes and hands.

Speechmark

Aims

* **To encourage and enable individuals to choose a medium to work with, from a range of options**
* **To offer the opportunity to experiment and practise with one medium, and to gain some confidence in its use.**

Materials

* **Art Resource Box**
* **Card/paper, cut in to 10 or 15cm squares**
* **Optional: other media not found in Art Resource Box, such as fabric paints or inks.**

Method

Spread out the materials and tools on a table. Ask each person to select only one medium that they would like to work with. Give each person three squares of card or paper, and ask them to make three different images, or 'marks', on each card, using only the medium they have chosen. Encourage people to think of different ways to use this medium – have a general discussion initially, if this helps. Ask people to use a different technique, and draw or paint spontaneously on each square. It can be a repeated image created in different ways, abstract or realistic, but done with the same medium. When they have finished, ask group members to spread their work out on tables or the floor. Encourage people to see how many different lines, shades, textures and styles were created, using just one medium.

What did people learn from the experience? Did they enjoy using the medium they chose? How easy/difficult was it to use? Would they use it again? If there is time, suggest that people select another medium, and repeat the exercise. When finished, work together to display the squares, on a wall or a piece of mount board, to create a montage. Encourage the group to decide where each square should go. Stick the squares on with BluTack® so that they can be rearranged where needed.

Alternatives

1   Look through books, or visit exhibitions, which features artists using the same medium in different ways.
2   Certain group members may want to further develop their skills and expertise using a single medium. Explore with them ways to achieve this, through books, videos, individual tuition, or by joining an art class.
3   Encourage people to keep a portfolio of their work, so that they can follow the development and progress made using their chosen medium.

Comments

Some people may have already found a medium they like to work with, and may want to stick with this. Where possible, encourage people to be a little more adventurous and try a new medium. If they choose not to, suggest they try as many different techniques/styles as they can, to stretch their imagination and find ways to use the medium creatively. Encourage group members to offer suggestions, and to inspire each other.

Aims

* **To explore and experience using mixed media to create images**
* **To work alongside others in order to inspire teamwork, communication skills, making choices and sharing ideas.**

Materials

* **Art Resource Box**
* **Magazines to cut up for collage, if needed**
* **Several large sheets of card or paper, A3 or larger**
* **Simple pictures/line drawings relating to a theme or subject, such as 'plants', 'animals', 'people', 'buildings' or 'boats'.**

Method

Spread out the mixed media, tools, magazines, scissors, PVA glue, and paper or card on a table near the work area. Separate group members into teams. Give out the title of a chosen theme – for example, 'animals' – and point out that there are pictures to look at to inspire and assist with shapes, colours and characteristics of animals. Ask each team to decide on an animal, and to select a sheet of card or paper and at least three different media from the table, as well as the tools they would like to use. Tell each team that they now have to discuss and decide how they are going to draw/paint their animal using the media they have chosen. They need to decide who does what, or work spontaneously together.

Encourage people to support each other as needed. If a member of the team is unable to participate physically, enable them to contribute verbally, or observe comfortably. When all the teams have finished, enjoy the finished work, and allow each team to talk about the animal chosen and the media they used. Encourage people to share what they learned from the experience.

Alternatives

1 This exercise can be repeated using several different themes, or one chosen by the team members.

2 Use still life, and ask the teams to recreate the same still life using media of their choice. Compare the work in a constructive way when they have finished.

3 Look through art books showing work by different artists, using a variety of media. Try making pictures based on the same theme as the artists, and using the same media. Compare the differences and similarities.

4 Visit art galleries or local art and craft shops, and study work by other artists or local people using mixed media. Note down ideas for future reference or experiments.

Comments

Avoid comparing the work done in teams, unless the group chooses to do so. Keep the session non-competitive and non-judgemental if possible. Create a positive atmosphere, in which ideas and experiences may be shared with confidence.

Printing

Aims

* To experience and create artwork using a variety of materials
* To create abstract images while experimenting with colour and shape.

Materials

* **Art Resource Box**
* **Paper, of different textures and sizes**
* **Card and scraps of fabric**
* **Collection of items to use as printing tools – for example, tissue paper, cling-film, aluminium foil; bubblewrap and other textured materials**
* **Small objects to print with – for example, corks, small blocks of wood, and small household items such as keys, cotton reels, chopsticks and beads**
* **Cardboard mount frames**
* **Lots of newspapers, old magazines, old sheets, plastic lids and large containers**
* **Soap, water, towels and protective clothing!**

Method

Before the group arrives, arrange several large containers of paint on a table covered with newspapers. Use primary colours (red, yellow, blue) and black and white. Cover other surfaces used with newspaper or old sheets. Ensure that everyone is wearing protective clothing, and that sleeves are rolled up! Have plenty of warm, soapy water nearby. Invite each person to select paper or card and place this on a wad of newspaper or magazine for padding. Ask people to select several items to print with.

Begin with a demonstration yourself, by making some patterns and shapes. For example, scrunch up some paper or rags, dip lightly into the pot of paint, and press on to the paper. Now select a cork, dip it into another colour, and stamp the shape on to the same paper. Encourage people to make random prints, and to choose materials and colours spontaneously. When the paints are dry, get everyone to move a card frame slowly over the work, and ask them to select a section that pleases them. Suggest that when they have found a section they like, they should stop and draw around the inside of the frame, then cut out the chosen piece to mount on card and display on a wall. Encourage people to select a few more sections to create a colourful, abstract exhibition. Keep any small pieces to tear up for use in collage if desired.

Alternatives

1   If your budget allows, purchase some ready-made printing blocks for specific themes or images – for example, snowflakes for winter images.
2   Encourage group members to make print marks with fingers, hands, feet and elbows. Wash thoroughly afterwards!

Comments

Offer assistance, where needed, for people with limited dexterity. Hold the paper down with masking tape to avoid it slipping. Tape or glue some materials on to the end of a long stick or paintbrush, to enable people to reach the table/paper from a wheelchair.

Aims

* **To enable group members to create their own 'printing blocks', and to select and use materials to express their individuality.**

Materials

* **Art Resource Box**
* **Corrugated cardboard, cut into 10cm squares**
* **Blocks of wood – off-cuts from DIY centres, or children's building blocks**
* **String, lace, washing-up pads and other textured materials.**

Method

Inform the group that they will be making printing blocks, which cannot be used until the glue has dried. Another session will be needed to use the blocks, once they have dried. Give a demonstration first by selecting a block of wood or thick corrugated card. Choose some string, spread the glue thickly over the surface of the corrugated card, and arrange the string on the glued surface to create any pattern or shape – for example, spirals, zigzags or random arrangements.

Get the group members to create more blocks by using other textured materials, such as lace or small pieces of bubblewrap. Suggest that people can cut out smaller shapes from the corrugated card, and mount these on to larger corrugated blocks, to give a layered texture. When the printing blocks are completed, get everyone to lay them out to dry in a safe corner of the workspace. Inform the group that,

Making Print Blocks (cont'd)

when the glue is dry, they will be able to paint over the textured surfaces using a brush, or by dipping the printing block into a tray of paint.

Explain that, to make the prints, they will need to press the printing blocks firmly on to blank sheets of paper, which have been taped to thick wads of newspaper or magazines with masking tape. Decide a time to complete the printing session (for example, in the afternoon or next week). If there is time in this session, discuss the different ways in which the prints could be used – for example, to make greeting cards and wrapping paper, or used with fabric paints to decorate T-shirts or other items of clothing.

Alternatives

1 Use other materials to enable group members to make printing blocks. Potatoes and erasers can be used, with patterns cut into the flat surfaces using a craft knife (prepare these yourself before the session). People can create blocks with self-hardening clay, by rolling out clay into small squares or round shapes. Use biscuit cutters to make the shapes, and make patterns on the clay surface with objects such as matchsticks, cotton buds, pencils, the edges of a ruler and coins. When these dry, group members can paint over the textured surface of the clay block to make a print.

2 Use thin polystyrene sheets 15 x 20cm – these are made especially for craft or printing. (Do not use ceiling tiles, which are thicker.) Use water-based block printing inks with a roller. Encourage people to draw patterns firmly on to the surface of the tile with a blunt pencil, then roll the ink over the patterned surface of the tile. They then need to place a thin sheet of paper over the inked surface, and rub over the surface of the paper thoroughly with the back of a wooden spoon or a cloth. They can then take the paper off carefully to admire the print.

3 Recycle unwanted place mats (found in most pubs or around the house), and use these as blocks. Glue string and small objects (such as buttons or old coins) on one side to create a textured surface with which to print.

Comments

Why not arrange a visit to, or sessions with, a local printer, or invite someone in to demonstrate their practice to the group? Printing is a specialist art, and it is well worth introducing group members to the technical, creative and inspiring methods that experienced printers use. Many people with disabilities have found printing to be a rewarding and productive art experience.

Aims

* **To explore and use found objects to create a print**
* **To stimulate the imagination, and encourage people to look beyond the obvious.**

Materials

* **Art Resource Box**
* **Card/paper (black and mixed colours)**
* **A variety of 'found' objects – for example, small pebbles, shells, twigs, dried leaves, cones, flower heads, net, string, and household items such as cling-film, foil, and lollipop sticks.**

Method

Ask group members to collect items found at home, in their garden and when out for walks, a week before the session. When they arrive, spread the found objects on a table near the workspace. Then get members to cover tables with newspaper, and protect themselves with aprons or old shirts; fix paper over folded newspapers or magazines with masking tape, and put paint in plastic containers. Encourage them to pick any colours they choose.

To make the prints, inform the group that they will need to dip the found objects into the paint, and press them firmly but gently on to the paper. They can use one object repeatedly to create patterns, or use a variety of objects to create an image that is abstract or recognisable. When the prints are dry, suggest that people tear around their images to create a ragged edge, and paste them on to a black or coloured card to display on walls.

Alternatives

1 Encourage people to create prints randomly, and see if an image can be identified in the print – for example, a bird, butterfly, face or landscape. They can then draw around this image with a marker pen, pastels or crayons.

2 Take the group for a walk to local places – the park, a beach, or a forest. Collect found objects together that may be useful for printing.

3 Have a light-hearted competition for the most unusual item found. Ask people to bring in a collection, and to share their findings with the group.

4 Use fruit and vegetables for printing. People can make printing blocks by cutting potatoes and apples in half, and by using other vegetables, such as leeks, onions and carrots. (Discourage people from eating the materials afterwards!)

Comments

Start a collection of found objects yourself, a week or so before facilitating this session, just to make sure that objects are available on the day. If possible, have a go at printing with them well before the session, to help build confidence and gain experience, if you have not done this before.

Collage

Aims

* **To explore, and enjoy, using paper when creating images**
* **To build a collage, and gain experience in using an alternative medium to paint or crayons.**

Materials

* **Art Resource Box**
* **A4 paper/card, mixed colours**
* **Magazines and scrap paper to cut up. (Geographical, nature and gardening magazines are good to use. Collect unwanted illustrated books/photographic magazines from charity shops and friends/relatives.)**
* **Tissue paper**
* **Samples of collage work**
* **Have some ideas for a theme or inspiration as standby.**

Method

Begin with a general discussion on what people understand as collage. Explain to the group that collage is a picture made by sticking different materials, such as paper, textiles, photographs and small objects, on to a surface. Encourage the group members to look at some of the samples selected. Ask people to choose a theme. If this is difficult, suggest they begin with something abstract, using colour and shapes randomly, and see what happens. If they choose to use a theme, suggest they start with a specific idea or word, or a cutting from the magazines – for example a fish, flower or house.

Encourage people to draw an outline to work from, or to develop the picture randomly and spontaneously. They can use card or paper as the base on which to stick the images, or draw the outline. Invite the group to cut out pictures from the magazines, and use tissue paper by tearing it into pieces. This can be layered on to the paper to add extra colour where needed. People can tear or cut the paper and images, and, if desired, separate the elements of the work into colours, textures, shapes and subject-matter, before they start the picture.

They can then start building the collage, spreading PVA glue either directly on to the paper/card base, or on to the back of the pieces to be stuck down. Suggest they place the torn up pieces next to each other on the base and/or layered to form the collage. They can then add a coat of PVA glue over the final picture, to paste down any loose edges and to form a varnish over the finished picture. The glue looks white to begin with, but dries clear: warn people about this, especially if they have not used the glue in this way before! Offer assistance, and share ideas in the group with anyone who is struggling. When everyone has finished, allow each person to talk about their work, and what they have learnt from the experience. Would they do anything different next time? What would they like to try next? Discuss how to display the completed work.

Alternatives

1 Visit the local library, galleries and craft shops for ideas.
2 Ask group members to collect interesting photographs of people they know, or places they have visited. Encourage them to photocopy the photographs, and cut up the copies to make a collage. This is a fun way to present special events, such as weddings, birthdays and holidays. If placed on mount cards these collages can be displayed – framed or unframed, they look equally effective.
3 Experiment with colour and themes. Be as wildly abstract or as realistic as people want to be.
4 Find simple line drawings, patterns or ready-made colouring/pattern books for people to 'fill in' with collage, if they are stuck for ideas.

5 Use the letters of the alphabet to inspire work. Encourage the group to collect as many images as possible beginning with the letter 'A', and create a surreal, abstract collage with this. They can layer the images until the whole sheet is filled, or hide images behind and inside others: have fun, and stimulate the imagination! People can also create other collages using the letter 'B', and so on. Suggest that they create a collage alphabet book. This could take a lifetime, but offers at least 26 more session ideas!

Comments

If possible, save any previous paintings/drawings by group members that they no longer want to keep, but are colourful and have interesting patterns and shapes.

These can be torn into small pieces and stored in boxes by group members in one session, and used for collage at a later date. Build a collection of unwanted pictures, books, wrapping paper and materials to use for collage with the group. If there is time in sessions, encourage people to separate these into categories, such as 'human', 'animals', 'colour', 'textures' and 'patterns', for future use. Have the group members collect ideas, and encourage them to search for and collect their own collage materials.

Paper and Paint

collage: paper and paint

Aims

* **To encourage a team spirit, and the sharing of ideas, by creating a communal picture using only paper and acrylic paint**
* **To experience and enjoy the process of using the two media in ways that stretch and challenge the imagination.**

Materials

* **Art Resource Box – use only the acrylic paint and PVA glue**
* **A3 card or thick paper**
* **Magazines and pictures for cutting out – select images based on a chosen theme, such as 'In the country', 'At the zoo', or 'A walk in the park'.**

Method

Decide on the theme with the group – for example, 'A walk in the park'. Ask group members to go through the magazines and pictures, and select/cut out images that relate to 'the park'. They can draw their own images if preferred, and cut these out. (Images might include dogs, people, boats on a lake, discarded litter, ice-cream, plants and a football.) Suggest that they choose some bizarre, humorous images as well, such as flying saucers, angels, funny faces or an odd shoe. They may wish to select fairly small images and, if needed, they can reduce some images using a photocopier.

Encourage the group to design a scene together. Suggest they imagine a park scene. They can paint in the sky, a lake, some trees, bushes or buildings, and paste the cut-out images anywhere in this park – for example, a face peering from a

The Art Activity Manual © Marylyn Cropley 2004

Speechmark

bush, an angel sitting on a cloud, a bottle in the grass, or a shoe on a wall. Inspire people to be imaginative, and enjoy the session.

When the work is dry, people can paint over the whole picture with a glaze, made from a mixture of a little paint, water and some PVA glue. This gives a hint of colour over the whole scene, and can slightly camouflage some of the images. Suggest they try different colours, and cover areas separately, rather than the whole picture. If too much paint is used, this can be wiped off quickly with a clean damp cloth, and the section may be gone over again, if necessary. When everything is dry, suggest that they go over the whole picture again with a light glaze: this seals the work, and acts as a varnish. It can also enhance the colours and glazes underneath. Acrylic paint dries very quickly, so if a serious mistake is made, it is possible to save the collage by painting over the mistake.

Enjoy the completed image with the group, and encourage people to take some time to observe and identify some of the images hidden in the picture. At a glance, the picture will look like a landscape of a park. When observed closely, the hidden images will reveal themselves.

Alternatives

1 As a back-up to facilitating these sessions, collect as many bizarre images as you can before sessions begin, to inspire ideas and assist the group. Something 'out of context' will make the picture interesting or funny.
2 Encourage people to create fantasy or traditional scenes, such as 'the magic forest', or 'Christmas in the lounge'.
3 Split the group into teams to work separately, preferably in separate rooms: they are not to show each other their work until they have all finished. Then, each team can try to find as many images as they can in the other teams' work.

Comments

This can be an enjoyable and fun exercise for the group members. As a facilitator, try to keep the sessions humorous and light-hearted.

Patch Pictures

patchwork paper

patchwork fabric

PVA

Aims

* **To experience using a variety of fabrics, instead of paper, to make a collage**
* **To enjoy working and experimenting with shape, pattern and colour, to create patch pictures.**

Materials

* **Art Resource Box**
* **A4 card**
* **A collection of fabrics of different colours and textures, cut into small shapes (squares, circles or triangles)**
* **Books showing samples of fabric collage and patch pictures.**

Method

Look through the books with group members, and talk about the way fabric patches have been used to create a picture. Note colours, patterns and textures used, and the subject-matter chosen. Discuss how the spaces are used in the picture. Is the overall composition balanced? Can they see movement? If so, how is this portrayed? Do the shapes and colours complement each other, or do they clash? Is the picture too complex, too simple, or just right? Encourage them to explain their answers.

Ask the group to select an idea, and choose the fabric that may best represent the idea. Ask people, individually or collectively, to create a picture based on the idea chosen, or to create an image of random colours and patterns. Point out that it is not necessary to fill the whole card with the fabric. The images can be

very simple, or more complex. It is important that the process is enjoyed in a relaxed atmosphere. Encourage the group to look at the finished work together, and to admire and enjoy their creations.

Alternatives

1 Suggest to members that they use fabric pens or marker pens to draw additional lines and images on to the patch collage, such as more detail in trees by drawing in the leaves. They can emphasise certain areas with gold or silver paint, or string, lace and threads, to create more texture and patterns.

2 Involve the group in an activity where they can only use black and white fabrics with shades of grey, and create silhouettes.

3 Encourage people to observe closely the subjects they wish to re-create in their pictures. Suggest that they spend time researching and developing a sketchbook of ideas. They could observe the shape of buildings, people, animals and trees, and also look for colours and textures that are not obvious at first glance. Remind them to keep a note of anything that would be useful for future work.

4 Instead of using PVA glue, use Velcro® pads, double-sided tape, or felt shapes on a felt background for less permanent or moveable pictures.

Comments

Using fabric for collage can be frustrating the first time round. Some materials may require more glue than others, and people may be unfamiliar with handling these materials, so you will need to give support with this activity initially.

A Tracing and Copying

Drawing

Aims

* **To explore and practise drawing lines and shapes, by tracing and copying**
* **To build confidence, and encourage group members who feel unable to draw freehand to make a start.**

Materials

* **Art Resource Box**
* **Tracing paper**
* **Carbon paper**
* **A4 white paper**
* **Photographs from books, magazines or personal collection**
* **Colouring books, or books with patterns/doodles.**

Method

Lay the books and photographs out on a long table near the workspace used by the group. Ask each member of the group to select an image from the collection, which they would like to copy or trace. Suggest that people have a go at copying their image by observation initially, using pencils or charcoal: they should copy the outline first, and fill in details later. If a person feels unable or unwilling to draw freehand, encourage them to try tracing.

Show the group how to place the tracing paper over the image, and hold it down with masking tape. Then encourage them to trace over the outline of the image seen through the tracing paper, with a sharp pencil, and assist as needed. Get

PART II: DRAWING

Speechmark

them to place the traced image over a blank sheet of paper, with the carbon paper sandwiched between (ink side facing down!), then go over the image on the tracing paper with a pencil or pen, to transfer a carbon copy on to the blank sheet. They can then draw over the outline of the traced image with a pen, pencil or crayon, and fill in the picture with colour or shading as desired.

Suggest that people have a go at tracing without the carbon paper – offer instructions if someone has not traced before. After tracing the image, they need to turn over the tracing paper, and follow the lines on the reverse by rubbing over them thoroughly with a soft pencil. Then turn the tracing paper back over, and place this on the blank sheet of paper. They will need to go over the image again with a pencil to transfer it on to the paper. If people are unfamiliar with tracing, it is better to get them to use very simple outlines and images to begin with. They can finally fill in the outlined picture as desired.

Alternatives

1 Encourage any nervous or potential artists to trace over an image several times first, then try drawing the same image freehand. They may be pleasantly surprised at how much they learnt through repetition and practice!

2 Instead of transferring the traced image on to another paper, suggest that people go over the lines with a thick, permanent black marker pen, and colour in with highlighter pens or brightly coloured felt-tip pens.

3 Encourage members to have a go at creating a stained glass window effect, by sandwiching the tracing paper between two frames of black card and colouring in lines of the image on the tracing paper with a black felt-tip pen.

4 It is possible to trace over images without using tracing paper, but having a bright light behind the image to be traced. This can be done by using a glass-topped table, with a lamp or bright torch shining up from underneath the table. Attach the image to the table with tape, and place a blank sheet of paper over this (again, securing it with tape if necessary). The light under the table will enable people to see the image through the paper clearly enough to trace, quickly and efficiently.

Comments

Tracing enables most people to copy any image they want, with as little or as much detail as they wish. It is a good way to build confidence and practise drawing skills. Larger images are helpful to people with limited sight, and those

Tracing and Copying (cont'd)

with limited dexterity. Use thicker pencils or marker pens to help someone to see the lines they draw.

If necessary, draw over original images with thick, felt-tip pen lines to enable someone to see them more clearly through the tracing paper: seeing someone with limited sight draw, when they once felt they would never draw again, makes this well worth the effort! Enlarge images by photocopying them up to A3 size. Household grease-proof paper, which comes on rolls, can be used to trace larger images.

PART II: DRAWING

Speechmark

Aims

* **To experiment with mixed media, and have the opportunity to explore preferences**
* **To gain more awareness of personal style and preferences, when choosing a specific 'tool' and when drawing.**

Materials

* **Art Resource Box**
* **A4/A3 paper – mixed textures and colours**
* **'Tools' other than pencils and brushes – for example, twigs, feathers, chopsticks and string**
* **Postcards, photographs and illustrated calendars for inspiration**
* **Tape recorder/CD player, and soft, gentle music.**

Method

Play the music softly in the background. Invite group members to choose a selection of tools and materials to work with. Ask them to begin by having a doodle to warm up. They can do this by drawing lines and shapes randomly, using different media and tools. After a few minutes, ask people to select a theme to work from. They can use the postcards and photographs for inspiration, or draw from imagination. If anyone gets stuck, ask them to try listening to the music with their eyes closed, and to imagine colours, lines and shapes inspired by the music.

They can try drawing the same image using different tools, or draw different images using the same tool, and compare the differences. Encourage people to stretch and challenge themselves, as long as they feel comfortable in this situation. Talk about the completed work, and discover which tools/media people enjoyed using, and why.

Alternatives

1   Rather than holding a practical session, encourage group members to look at books and videos on freehand drawing.

2   Invite experienced artists in to do demonstrations, or to work on a specific skill with the group.

3   Take group members to visit places of interest to get ideas, and encourage people to draw. Advise them to use a sketchbook regularly, and to keep it for future reference. Emphasise that regular practice is necessary to improve drawing skills.

4   Think of fun and unusual ways to draw. Get group members to use fingers and toes to draw with, or use body paints to draw on themselves!

Comments

It is important to stress that drawings do not have to be an exact copy of the original. However, if people want to develop their drawing skills further, they may need help and encouragement to find ways to achieve this. Encourage people to find out about local tutors/art classes that teach drawing skills.

Aims

* **To explore and enjoy the experience of drawing**
* **To build confidence and observation skills while drawing a still life**
* **To understand the value of using a sketchbook, and to practise drawing.**

Materials

* **Art Resource Box**
* **Sketchbooks or ring binders (A4/A5), with drawing paper that has been hole-punched appropriately**
* **Objects for still life drawing – simple forms such as vases, plants, pebbles and fruit**
* **Black or white paper or card on which to place objects**
* **Still life drawings and sketches by other artists.**

Method

Before the group arrives, set up a few objects on a table in the centre of the room. Place the objects on the black or white card. When the session begins, invite members to rearrange the objects if they wish. Encourage people to walk/move around the objects, and observe carefully. Ask them to find a position to sit, from where they can draw the objects comfortably, and at the angle they prefer.

Talk for a short while about the objects on the table. Ask people to describe the shapes, size and textures seen. Where does the light fall on the objects, and where is its source? Where are the shadows and the darkest/lightest tones? Talk about the colours: do they complement each other, or do they clash? Get people to look at the size and shape of the objects, then select some paper or an appropriately sized sketchbook to accommodate the image chosen.

Encourage people to sketch the outlines first, then select the darkest, lightest and mid tones. They can practise shading in with lines, cross-hatching, or using the side of the pencils to block in areas. Tell them to be bold, and to leave the lightest areas white and the darkest black. Try to avoid comparisons, and reassure group members that their drawings do not have to be exact replicas of the original. Allow people to work at their own pace.

When the sketches are finished, offer options to leave them as they are, or to draw over with pens and other media. Suggest that people keep the work in sketchbooks, or store it in the ring binders.

Alternatives

1   Have several objects ready, but only display them one at a time. Encourage people to draw each one as quickly as possible, before it is changed for the next one. Allow about two or three minutes for each sketch (or longer, depending on the ability of group). Use objects such as driftwood, seaweed and shells.
2   Go outdoors together and draw something 'still' – a tree, or gate or large stone. Use charcoal or pastels to draw with. Try white pastels/chalk on black paper, and suggest that people try drawing what they see by highlighting the lightest areas only.
3   Encourage people to look at spaces between the objects and try drawing these only.
4   Get group members to draw objects using only straight lines – this can be difficult at first, so provide rulers if you have to!

Comments

Encourage people to keep their sketches, and come back to these at a later date to create a picture, using their sketches as a reference. Collect information and simple instructions on how to draw still life, or encourage people to consider local classes if they are interested in developing these skills.

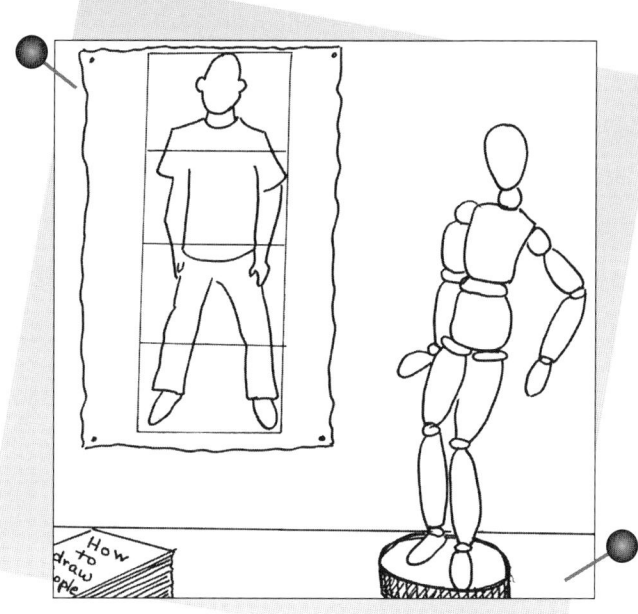

Aims

* **To build confidence, and encourage group members to have a go at drawing people**
* **To enable observation and understanding of the diverse shapes and forms of the human body.**

Materials

* **Art Resource Box**
* **Sketchbooks**
* **Photographs of people, showing the whole body**
* **Tracing and drawing paper**
* **'Lay figure' (a small, jointed, wooden figure)**
* **Art books showing works by different artists, from different periods and cultures, all depicting the human figure.**

Method

Look through the art books with the group, and have a general discussion on how artists have portrayed the human figure. Ask people to look at the photographs that show the human figure in full. Invite people to select a photograph, tracing paper, drawing paper/sketchbook, and to have a go at tracing around the body of the person/people in the photograph. Advise them to ignore the details, and concentrate only on the outline of the body.

Then ask them to draw outlines around the body shapes as if they were enclosing them in boxes: suggest that they draw rectangles, squares or triangles

around the body. This will depend on the position of the body, and what shape they think the body is making. Then ask people to draw a line half way across the box shape, as if they were 'cutting the body in half'. They then need to do the same to the top and bottom half of the boxes, so that the body has been divided into quarters within the box-shaped outline. Encourage them to practise this a few times with different figures. Have a general discussion on what shapes naturally emerged when 'boxing in' the figures, and the diversity of shapes found when drawing the human figure.

If a wooden lay figure is available, use this to observe and discuss the overall shape and proportion of the human figure, and how this can be divided into sections. Invite people to have a go at drawing the lay figure. Place the figure in any position, and start by drawing the overall shape first. More details, such as features and clothes, can be added later if desired. Remind people that practice makes perfect, and not to worry if they do not get the figures as they want. Have a go at turning some of the shapes into cartoon characters or funny people, to add some humour to the occasion.

Alternatives

1 If the group members are willing, encourage them to explore their own bodies. Suggest that they measure each other with a tape-measure or string. Compare sections of the body – for example, the length from head to shoulder, shoulder to waist, waist to knees and knees to feet. Ask them to observe how people's bodies differ in shape and size, and also the similarities.
2 If they are feeling brave, encourage people to sit as models (fully clothed!), and have a go at drawing each other.
3 Use a theme: after drawing the lay figure, or after tracing body outlines, get the group to fill in the details to create different characters, such as vicars, old men, old women, dancers, people at work or people at play.
4 Encourage members to go out and about, to observe people and develop a sketchbook. Invite them to have fun drawing stick people, carrot-shaped people, and cartoon characters.

Comments

If someone is keen to develop life-drawing skills further, consider local art classes, using professional models.

Aims

* **To use the diversity and wonder of nature to inspire and motivate people to produce artwork**
* **To enable people to identify a part of nature that they like to draw or paint.**

Materials

* **Art Resource Box**
* **Pictures/photographs showing landscape**
* **Paintings and drawings of landscapes by different artists**
* **Drawing paper/sketchbooks**
* **Card frames – purchase these from art or craft shops and frame makers, or you could even make some with the group.**

Method

Look at the pictures of the landscapes with the group. Talk about what they see in the pictures. Study the composition. Ask people what they first saw when they looked at the picture. What else made them look at the picture further? How pleasing was the image to the eye? Where is the horizon in the picture: is it too high, too low or just right? How is the picture divided? Is it balanced? Are there other features such as people, rivers, roads and fences? Are they 'moving into' the picture or 'moving outwards'? Does this work for the picture?

Nature *(cont'd)*

If possible, go for a short walk with the group, and find a view. Using the card frame, encourage people to take it in turns to hold this up against the view, and move it around until a part of the landscape is framed that is pleasing and balanced to the viewer. Encourage people to consider similar points as before. What is seen? Where is the horizon? What catches the eye first? Allow members to make some sketches, if possible.

Return to the workspace, and offer people the opportunity to have a go at drawing a landscape. Advise them to keep the lines simple, and to consider some of the points raised in previous discussions. If people are nervous about drawing in this way, suggest that they try tracing over the pictures collected first, until they feel more confident. Try tracing with a pencil, and going over the pencil lines with ink pens.

Alternatives

1   Have some colouring books with line drawings of landscapes as a standby for people to colour in, if they are unable or reluctant to draw.
2   Encourage people to assist and support each other. One can draw the outlines, while another colours in the details.
3   Explore other parts of nature in a similar way to the landscape session: try studying animals, plants, trees, sky, clouds, sea, rivers and lakes. Take people out as often as possible to experience nature in the flesh.
4   Have a theme, and encourage people to do as many sketches as they can on the one subject.
5   Visit places of interest, nature reserves, gardens, zoos and aquariums. Sketch what is seen, or take photographs and collect brochures, and work from these in the next session.

Comments

Nature is a truly inspiring subject for any artist. However, some adults with certain disabilities only get the chance to observe nature through books, television and a nearby window. Every artist needs to experience nature in the raw, and in all its glory. It is important that a group facilitator does everything in their power to facilitate this opportunity for every person with whom they work.

Sara's dream
I dreamt I was a mermaid
With long curls and flowing hair.
My friends were creatures
of the sea:
a watery world
we share...

Imagine!

Aims

* **To offer an opportunity to be creative and use the imagination when creating a work of art**
* **To find sources of inspiration that trigger and inspire the imagination.**

Materials

* **Art Resource Box**
* **Paper**
* **A selection of ideas to inspire/motivate people – for example, short, descriptive poems, or articles that give brief descriptions of scenes, people, characters and feelings.**
* **Paintings/illustrations by other artists, showing images that are surreal or fantastic – illustrations from children's books of fairy tales, myths and folklore can be very useful.**

Method

Look at the paintings and illustrations together, and have a general discussion about them. Ask people to consider if the artists used their imaginations, and if so, in what way? Select a short poem or article for the group, and ask people to close their eyes while you read it out slowly. Invite people to try to imagine the scene/characters as the poem is being read to them, and to visualise what they

Imagination (cont'd)

hear. When you have finished, encourage the group to write a list of words that describe what people 'saw'. Do this as a group, or individually if preferred.

Read the poem again, and ask people to draw what they see. (Use the written list of words to help if needed.) Reassure people that the images do not have to be exactly as they imagined. They can even change what they draw as they go along. Set the imagination free, and 'go with the flow'! Encourage people to be spontaneous, work at their own pace, and to create as many images as they wish to, or have time for.

Alternatives

1 Suggest that group members make up their own short story or poem. Encourage them to collect their own ideas before the session, and start a scrapbook of ideas. Use scene-setting phrases to inspire ideas – for example, 'a walk in the park', 'standing on the beach', 'looking out of the window', or 'looking in the mirror'. (Be aware that some images may take people by surprise, and may be upsetting. Have a contingency plan to offer support, should the need arise.)

2 Play some interesting music, ask people to listen for a while, and then encourage them to make a picture inspired by the music.

3 Ask group members to design an illustration for a folk tale, pantomime or myth.

4 Encourage people to pick out an interesting character from a magazine. Draw or cut out the person from the magazine, and transfer the figure on to a blank sheet of paper. Suggest that people create their own scene round this person.

5 Suggest keeping a sketchbook to draw, or describe in words, any dreams people have had, or have heard about from others. They can try to interpret these dreams in a creative way if they wish.

Comments

Using the imagination can be difficult. If anyone is struggling with this, do a little exercise by hiding something they have not seen, in your hand or in a box – for example, a ring, an apple, or a watch that belongs to someone else in the group. Ask the person to try to imagine what might be in your hand or the box. Give one or two clues if absolutely necessary! Continue this exercise in various ways by getting people to take it in turns to imagine what might be in different places in the room – for example, in John's pocket, in Mary's handbag, or in a carrier bag in the corner of the room.

PART II: DRAWING

Speechmark

Paintings

Aims

* **To explore the outcome of using paint thickly or thinly**
* **To identify a preference when using paints – for example, watercolour (thinly), or acrylics (thickly)**
* **To explore and practise using the diverse textures of paint when thick or thin, and to enjoy the process of painting.**

Materials

* **Art Resource Box**
* **Paper or canvas for watercolours or acrylics**
* **Hairdryer (optional).**

Method

Encourage people to use only acrylics. Remember that acrylic paint dries very quickly, and is permanent once dried. Warn the group, and advise them to use protective clothing: have warm, soapy water and towels nearby! Have some water in spray bottles, as this will help to keep the paint moist when it is sprayed on to the palette at frequent intervals. (Wash brushes well afterwards, and keep them wet throughout the session.) Inform the group that acrylic paint can be used thickly, straight from the tube, or thinly, mixed with water, or water and PVA glue. PVA used with a small amount of paint can give a pleasing, glazed effect, when painted over a dry layer of paint.

Suggest that people begin painting by first covering the surface of the paper with a mixture 'wash' of paint and water, using water generously to dilute the paint. This should dry fairly quickly, but a hairdryer may speed up the process if you have one available. They can then use a second layer of paint (of a different colour), if desired. When this is dry, suggest that they use thick acrylic paint, with little or no water, to create lines, patterns and texture on top of the base colour(s). Enjoy the process, encouraging people to continue to experiment, using the paint thinly or thickly. Display finished work, or keep it for creating interesting, textured paper pieces in collage.

Alternatives

1 Encourage group members to experiment with other media, such as oil paints, poster paints or powder paints. Have them experiment with watercolours by mixing the paint very thinly with water, and creating an initial wash on the paper/canvas. Layer over with further washes when dry, and ensure that the bottom layer is dry before adding the next layer otherwise the paints may mix and start to look 'muddy'. Encourage people to make single, sweeping strokes with the paint, and then leave to dry, rather than repeatedly moving the brush forwards and backwards till the paint loses its colour and the paper begins to tear, which has been known to happen!

2 Look at books and videos that demonstrate the techniques for using paint thickly or thinly. Use various tools, such as knitting needles, pencils and matchsticks, to 'scratch' through the layers of thick paint, creating interesting textures, patterns and colours, which are visible through the layers. Use a plastic chopping board, and squeeze a few blobs of paint on to it. Create patterns and textures by working the paint around the board with the fingertips, and 'save' the patterns by making a print. Place a sheet of blank paper over the work before it dries, press gently but firmly, and lift the paper carefully to reveal a pattern. This is a messy business, but it is fun!

Comments

Ensure that people wash the brushes well in hot soapy water, as well as scraping unused acrylic paint from the palette and washing thoroughly. Alternatively, store unused paint under plastic cling-film, to keep it slightly damp.

Experimenting with Paint

Aims

* **To offer the opportunity to paint freely, and enjoy the learning process**
* **To create a relaxed environment that will inspire people to paint spontaneously, and to work as a team.**

Materials

* **Art Resource Box**
* **Large sheets of paper**
* **Access to water**
* **Protective clothing, newspapers, and paper towels**
* **Unusual tools, such as feathers, cotton buds and twigs**
* **Tape recorder and tape – use soothing music.**

Method

Set out a variety of paints for the group to use – for example, poster paints, acrylics and watercolours. (Remind people to use different brushes or tools for each paint, and to wash thoroughly afterwards). Spread paper on the floor or a large table. Put the music on, and ask people to listen for a few minutes. Invite the group to work together to create a communal piece of work, an abstract inspired by the music.

Encourage people to select paint randomly, and to use it thickly or thinly to create patterns and shapes, as well as blocks of colour. Use brushes of different lengths and thickness, and the other more unusual tools set out. Enjoy and explore the processes of painting and teamwork. Display the finished work as it is, or cut into smaller pieces when dry, to use for collage, or for making cards or calendars.

Alternative

When the paint has dried, group members can return to the work and outline shapes or patterns with other media, such as ink pens, pastels, gold, silver or felt-tip pens, and can create some stunning effects.

Comments

If people find it difficult to work as a team, enable them to work individually, and to have the opportunity to share their anxieties. Not everyone is able to share space or work when doing art: people can become quite possessive of their creations, and may not realise this until faced with such an exercise. Be respectful of this, and encourage group members likewise. Validate feelings, and allow for time out, or for people to walk away to do their 'own thing'.

Aims

* **To experience using mixed media with paint**
* **To create tiles, and enjoy the variety of textures and colour that can be produced with mixed media and paint.**

Materials

* **Art Resource Box**
* **Thick card or hardboard cut into squares of 20 x 20cm**
* **Materials for collage – for example, dried beans, lentils, string, net, dried leaves, flowers, thin bark from trees, wood shavings, dried tea leaves, unwanted dry herbs, glitter, or anything else that is not too heavy or bulky**
* **Samples of designs and images to copy from, if needed.**

Method

Set out the acrylic paint and PVA glue in containers, preferably before the group arrives. Ask each person to choose a card or a piece of hardboard, and encourage them to select some of the collage materials set out. Ask the group to arrange a pattern/design on the square card or hardboard in front of them with the materials chosen. Point out the samples of designs and images, if they need something to copy from, or added inspiration. They can then draw a pattern on the card first and fill in the relevant spaces using PVA glue, before adding the materials to make a collage on each card. This will give a variety of textured surfaces.

Patterns and textures can vary from card to card, or have similarities. Demonstrate if needed. Suggest that they leave the squares to dry, and then paint over with the acrylic paint. (This will also act as a varnish/glue to hold the materials on the cards.) People may add other colours over the first to create a glazed effect if desired, or mix colours while the cards are still wet to create interesting swirls and patterns. Enable the group to create a colourful, textured montage with the cards when dry.

Alternatives

1   Adding gold or silver paint to the collage can also be very effective. Suggest that people could add quick dabs of paint when the base paint is wet to give an interesting blend, or highlight the card here and there when paint is dry.

2   They could paint all the squares/collage with white only, or another single colour. For a festive tiled wall, try spraying all the tiles gold and silver.

3   Suggest a theme for the montage – for example, an underwater scene, using shells (crushed if necessary) and fish shapes made with string or other materials.

Comments

When using beans and pulses, it may be necessary to use a lot of PVA glue, and to varnish the completed work when dry, to ensure that all the materials are anchored securely.

Finished Work

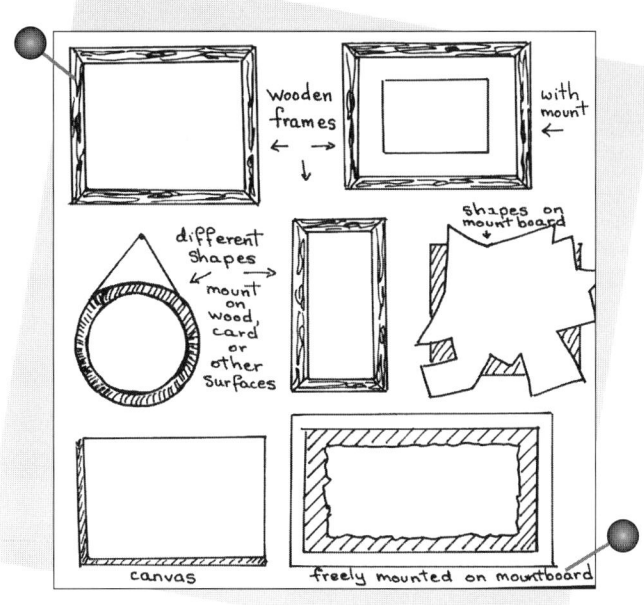

Aims

* **To discuss and share views on the presentation of completed artwork**
* **To identify personal preferences on how work can be framed or presented**
* **To experiment by presenting and/or framing a piece of artwork.**

Materials

* **Art Resource Box**
* **White or black mount cards, cut into 50cm squares**
* **Frames and mount card, ready cut, in different sizes and colours**
* **A selection of artwork created by group members**
* **Catalogues and brochures from galleries/art shops showing framed works of art.**

Method

Look through the catalogues and brochures with the group. Observe and discuss the different ways in which the pictures have been framed. How does a frame help to enhance a picture? Which type of frame did group members like/dislike? Is it always necessary to frame a picture? What alternatives are there? Look through the work done by the group, and ask people to select a few pieces to mount or frame. Some pictures may need to be cut down to size or trimmed: warn the group about this.

Ask people to observe while you select the frames and the black/white mount boards, and place different pieces of their work behind the frames or on the mount boards (leaving a wide margin all round). Ask group members to choose the frame or mount that best suits the piece of work they have chosen. Encourage them to consider why that frame or mount looks best, and if the colour/tone of the mount/frame enhances or detracts from the picture chosen.

You may find that none of the frames/mounts will suit a specific picture. If so, discuss why that is. When everyone has agreed on the mount/frame to use, enable members to cut the picture to size, if necessary, and glue it on to the mount, or sandwich it between the frame and backing card. Discuss where to display the work, collectively or individually.

Alternatives

1 Visit galleries and art shops with the group to explore and gain awareness of the variety of ways in which work can be framed or presented. It is well worth visiting modern art galleries and shops, and comparing new ways of framing with those used by the 'old masters'. Discuss the visits, and the preferences people had for the way certain pictures were framed.
2 Invite a skilled picture framer in to do a demonstration/talk about the art of framing.
3 Encourage people to join workshops on framing technique and mounts.

Comments

Ready-made frames can be purchased at low cost from some discount stores. Alternatively, look around charity shops or car boot sales for interesting frames to recycle. They can be cleaned, rubbed down, and repainted in different ways, to suit the picture. Glass can be removed, and the frames used for more permanent pictures done with acrylic paint. Glass will be needed for any work that needs protection, such as watercolour paintings, pastel works and charcoal sketches.

Aims

* To explore and discuss the different ways in which art has been displayed in homes, exhibitions, the workplace and the local community
* To encourage group members to value finished work, and gain the confidence and motivation to find a 'home' or outlet for their own work.

Materials

* Places to visit that exhibit works of art in the local community – for example galleries, libraries, restaurants, workplaces and homes
* Room for general discussion after the visit
* Examples of exhibitions, galleries and other public/ private places that exhibit work
* Ideas and suggestions for group members to consider as outlets to display work, such as local projects in which they could participate.

Method

Visit local places of interest that offer a variety of exhibition spaces showing different works of art. Consider the options, such as galleries, libraries, local restaurants, art shops, other public places and each other's homes! Ask the group to select one of these places, and have a general discussion on how artwork is

displayed in this place, and if the space used enhances or detracts from the picture. Is the display too cluttered? Is the lighting helpful? Can the work be viewed easily by others, and are the pictures suited to the space/environment they occupy?

Ask the group to consider where they would best like to display their own work, if the opportunity arose. Consider a variety of options. Spend some time researching local projects or exhibition spaces that would be available for group members to display their work. Would people be interested in having their own exhibition? If so, how would they do this, and where would it be? Consider joining or working with local art societies, or see if the library offers exhibition spaces. (You could also try local cafés, pubs and craft shops.) Be bold! People may prefer a more private space within their own homes or establishments. However, give people the final choice – even to say 'No' to displaying their work!

Alternative

Not everyone wants to display their work, and it is important to validate this. If it is due to a lack of confidence/experience, start gently by encouraging people to find a private space to hang their work – for example, in their bedroom, lounge, kitchen or conservatory.

Comments

Some people will be very keen to find exhibition space, but this may not always be as straightforward as it seems. However, it is well worth encouraging – where there is a will, there is a way! – and this will build confidence, self-esteem and motivation. Seek advice and suggestions from local societies, galleries and cultural services: the first step is important.

Aims

* **To explore and identify ways to store the work completed by group members**
* **To encourage individuals to begin building a personal portfolio**
* **To encourage people to value and appreciate the work they do, in the present and for the future, to build confidence and self-esteem.**

Materials

* **Art Resource Box**
* **Large sheets of strong paper or card – black, white and of various colours**
* **Staples and binding tape**
* **Work that people want to keep**
* **Tissue paper/thin paper**
* **Cardboard frames.**

Method

Encourage people to look through their work and decide what they want to keep. See if parts of an unwanted picture can be rescued by assisting people to cut out sections that they like. Suggest that people move a card frame over the picture to help identify a section that they may want to cut out and keep. If anyone is in doubt about disposing of a certain picture, suggest that it is kept and looked at again, at a later date. Any work that is fragile and easily damaged can be mounted on card, or stored in clear sleeves.

Ensure that works made with charcoal or pastels are 'fixed' by an appropriate varnish, and protected from smudging by covering with tissue paper or similar. Encourage people to make a portfolio by folding a large sheet of paper or card in half and stapling the sides, leaving the top end open. Ensure they cover the sides again with binding tape, to avoid scratches from the staples. If preferred, they can fold the paper so that there is an overlap at the open end, to make a large envelope with a flap. The portfolio can be named and decorated as desired, using the person's favourite medium. If possible, store portfolios flat on shelves, or in drawers or large boxes.

Alternatives

1   If people are keen and can afford it, they might enjoy investing in a strong portfolio, which can be purchased in most art shops. It is a good idea to shop around or buy one second-hand. Some discount shops sell art goods at very reasonable prices.

2   Look in charity shops and car boot sales for bags that can be adapted to make portfolios, and encourage group members to do the same.

3   Ask people to keep their sketchbooks, and store them in boxes for future reference.

4   Recycle large envelopes to store/separate and catalogue work. Collect flat boxes with lids for storing smaller work: boxes used for photographic paper are useful for this, as are the boxes that contain clear plastic sleeves purchased from stationery suppliers. If people have too much work and want to throw it away, but still to keep some form of record, this can be done by reducing it first to A4 size or smaller on a photocopier. Photocopied versions can then be stored in clear plastic sleeves in files, or in photographic albums. You may also photograph work using a camera, if the group has access to one. If possible, scan work and store it on computer/discs.

Comments

It is helpful to remember to put a name and date on the work, and to give it a title.

Evaluation

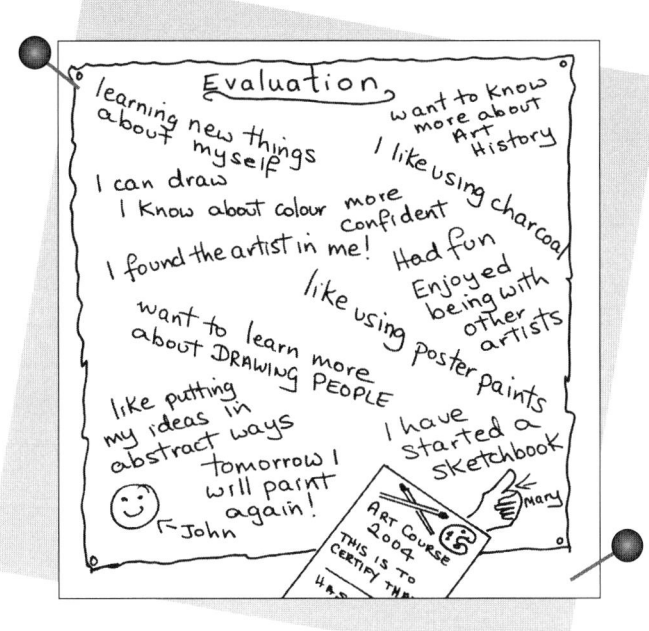

Aims

* **To offer group members the opportunity to evaluate previous sessions, and to identify the strengths and needs highlighted in these experiences**
* **To identify positive outcomes from the sessions (individually and collectively) and build a sense of achievement**
* **To record achievement by designing a personal award that is visual and can be displayed if desired.**

Materials

* **Paper, pens and felt-tip pens**
* **Flipchart, boards, or a large sheet of paper on which to write.**

Method

At the end of a series of sessions, take some time out to evaluate and appreciate the work created by the group. Discuss, and evaluate together, sessions covered to date. What did people gain from these activities? What new skills did they learn? Was it difficult/easy, and has it motivated them to continue exploring the world of art? What did people learn about art, and about themselves as artists?

Enable people to identify strengths and needs, in terms of knowledge on art and skills used. Also look at personal aspirations and expectations: were these achieved? If not, how can this be done in the future? Ask people what support they think they need in order to continue with their interest in art, such as learning new skills, more knowledge, information or opportunities.

Create a certificate together, and decide what to say on it to celebrate completion of the sessions and group members' achievements. Ask group members to design a logo/image for the certificate. Photocopy the completed certificate, and give each person in the group a copy with their name and signature on it.

Alternatives

1   Celebrate the end of the course with a small party, or have a trip/meal out.
2   Create a mini exhibition: look at and admire some of the work completed, privately or with family and friends, and evaluate progress and achievements together.
3   Invite individuals to give a short presentation to the group, by selecting one or two of their favourite pieces of work, and talking about the work they have completed. Encourage discussion about what they think they have learnt and achieved from the experience.

Comments

End on a positive note: some artists can be very vulnerable and nervous about their own abilities, and could very easily give up. That would be a shame! Evaluating and celebrating the end of a series of workshops can be very important to group members, especially as they may have developed strong friendships, and been a source of motivation for each other throughout the sessions. Suggest that people may like to meet from time to time, if appropriate, in order to continue to maintain contact. They may want to inspire each other as artists, and develop new friendships.

Aim

* **To share experiences and preferences learned from previous sessions, and to identify a way forward/the next step.**

Materials

* **Flipchart and pens**
* **Paper**
* **Information (if possible) on art courses and activities available in the local community/colleges. You could check with your local library, adult education centre and local art societies/galleries for programmes and classes available to the general public. Some offer special needs support and befriending schemes.**

Method

Have a general discussion on what people feel they have achieved from the sessions. Ask people to consider the 'gaps' in their learning, and any skills they would like to develop further. Decide if group members would like to continue with more sessions (if this is possible) and, if so, what would they like to cover in these sessions.

B 'Where to Next?' (cont'd)

Write down some ideas, and create a new programme. Ask people to consider activities available in the community that may help to cater for some of the needs of the group. Help to fill in application forms or make further enquiries if needed.

Alternatives

1   As well as local activities, be adventurous and consider activities further away, such as residential weekends, day trips to galleries/exhibitions, and a weekend trip to places where there are numerous galleries and sources of inspiration.
2   Research any grants/funding available for art projects – check with local authorities, cultural services and libraries for ideas and inspiration. Do not forget to look at the internet if you can.
3   Why not use the project ideas in this book for further sessions and inspiration?

Comments

All too often, people with disabilities have found themselves institutionalised, placed in centres or offered services that limit their fields of experience and scope for adventure. Many people's experiences stop at groupwork activities, and they become dependent on others to make things happen for them.

There is nothing wrong with groupwork – especially not if this experience has enabled individuals to gain the confidence and self-esteem to see themselves as individual artists in their own right, as well as sharing their love or new found discovery of art with other like-minded people. However, make sure that you encourage group members to value and accept their right to be considered as individual artists when they look to the future, and hopefully they will look forward to new experiences that incorporate this wholesome perception of themselves.

This page may be photocopied for instructional use only. *The Art Activity Manual* © Marylyn Cropley 2004

PART II: EVALUATION

Project Ideas

PART III

Project Ideas

The Four Seasons

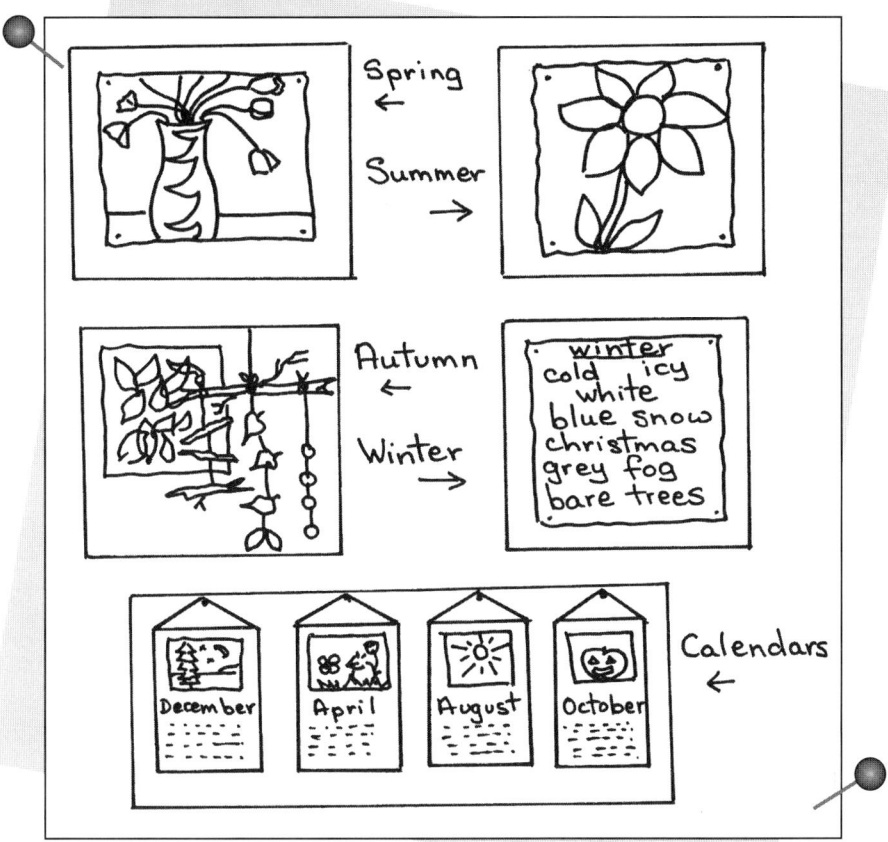

The seasons are an excellent source of inspiration for all artists. Nature, in all its glory, shows the cycle of life from birth to death. It offers rich presentations of colour, texture, light and form, and is constantly evolving, thus giving inspiration to artists for realistic and abstract work all the year round. Every aspect of nature changes – from plants, trees, skies, landscapes and weather, to insects and animals – a challenge for any artist! Project 1 is a free resource, which offers inspiration for art activities that can be developed at any time in the year, or as a continuous series of seasonal projects lasting a whole year, culminating with a project on making calendars.

Spring

Aim

* **To enable group members to identify aspects of spring that inspire and motivate them to be creative, and produce artwork individually or collectively.**

Materials

* **Art Resource Box**
* **Pictures, photographs, books, plants and information on spring – for example, a vase of daffodils, and pictures of crocuses or lambs and calves in a field**
* **Flipchart and pens.**

Method

Begin with a general discussion on spring. List words that people use to describe spring on a flipchart. Talk about changes in nature: the discussion can include what people actually see, or abstract thoughts such as imaginings and feelings. If possible, set up a still life such as a spring flower – daffodils go down well! Encourage group members to paint or draw what they see, figuratively or in an abstract form, picking out colours and shapes only. Offer alternatives, such as looking at photographs/pictures, or encourage people to create their own interpretations of spring.

Alternatives

1 Begin a seasonal sketchbook to record words and images inspired by reflections on spring. Use this to influence a larger piece of work at a later date.

2 Take the group on walks, or visit places of interest, such as gardens, fields and woodlands, to observe spring in action, while collecting notes for the sketchbooks. Collect found objects or interesting plants to bring to a still life session.

3 Suggest a theme linked to spring, such as 'birth', 'new beginnings', 'animals', 'plants' or 'landscapes', on which group members can base their work.

4 Consider festivals or public events that happen at this time of the year, and develop a project around these.

Comments

Spring is a very colourful and inspiring time of the year for many artists. Use this season to inspire group members to have a fresh start, and a fresh look at their own abilities and perception of themselves as artists.

Aims

* **To consider how summer can inspire and influence artwork**
* **To look at works by other artists that are influenced by summertime, and to create work in a similar style, or inspired by the same title.**

Materials

* **Art Resource Box**
* **A collection of pictures by various artists that were inspired by summer – encourage members to bring their own examples to the session.**

Method

Display the collection of pictures around the workspace, either on available wall space, display boards or tables, before the group arrives. Encourage the group to study the work of other artists, and to discuss how the work is influenced or inspired by the theme of summer. They can consider the different aspects of summer covered, such as the beach, flowers in sunlight, people bathing, and sunflowers. Next, ask people to select a picture they like or find interesting, and create an image based on the style or title of their chosen picture.

Alternatives

1 Hold activities outdoors. Arrange group visits to local places (or further afield) to paint and draw, or take photographs.
2 Encourage group members to continue the seasonal sketchbook.
3 Suggest that group members design a summer outfit, paint/print a T-shirt, or complete a study on wildlife – insects, bugs or butterflies are good topics for this.

Comments

Summertime is rich with colour, light, activities and scenes. Think about activities that take place in summer and the places people go for their holidays. Collect postcards and photographs to use in sessions, and enable group members to re-create these scenes figuratively or as abstracts.

Aims

* **To explore and admire the colours, textures and natural beauty of autumn**
* **To use found objects to inspire artwork.**

Materials

* **Art Resource Box**
* **Collection of natural found objects, such as leaves, twigs, seeds, nuts and cones.**

Method

Begin the project by inviting group members to talk about the beauty and richness of autumn, when nature sheds its leaves, and change is in the air. Encourage them to consider the colours of autumn, in the leaves, sky and sunsets. Suggest that they have a go at creating a mobile or textured collage with the found objects, and paint the work with the colours of autumn.

Alternatives

1   To obtain the maximum inspiration from autumn, go out as often as possible with the group. Walk through woods, over fields and in the park at different times in the day: early mornings and evenings are good times. It does not always have to be as a group – suggest that individuals try this, either on their own, or with family/friends.

2   'Change' is a key word for autumn. Use this as a theme to inspire other projects. Study sunsets, early morning atmospheres, and changes to trees and landscapes. Take photographs, or make sketches and notes.

3   As you walk through the woods or fields, use nature to create a sculpture or a piece of 'land art'. Celebrate seasonal events that occur in autumn. Create paintings and drawings, or sculptures, inspired by these events.

Comments

Encourage people to capture the colours and atmosphere of autumn, by making notes in their sketchbooks with drawings and/or the written word. Recommend that they use their sketchbooks frequently, preferably on a daily basis.

Aim

* **To use colours, textures, lines and patterns inspired by winter.**

Materials

* **Art Resource Box**
* **Photographs, pictures, books and words showing different aspects of winter**
* **A large sheet of paper.**

Method

Have a general discussion on winter with the group, and write out a list of words together to describe this season. Ask people to look at the pictures collected, and suggest that they may be useful as inspiration for group members to create their own pictures describing winter. Encourage them to consider winter colours: are they cold or warm? Encourage them to look at the simple structures and frameworks left in nature once autumn passes, such as the shape of naked trees, bushes and landscapes.

Suggest that group members think about how people change in terms of fashion, and what they do in winter. Look at local gardens and natural surroundings. Encourage people to think about the essence of winter – the mist, dew, snow, cold, dark evenings and very bright sunlight. Now ask them to re-create what they have seen and felt in any way they like. There are no set rules!

Alternatives

1 If there is snow, use this to inspire the group to create sculptures and land art. Enjoy 'drawing' on snow with twigs and footprints.
2 Use seasonal events to inspire further art projects.
3 If it is too cold to go out, ask people to sketch what they see through windows, from different angles and places.

Comments

Nature can be very still and beautiful at this time of the year. Encourage the group to make the most of it – to go out and take pictures, make quick sketches, and to discover interesting areas in the garden, park and woods, that have suddenly been revealed by the passing of autumn and the onset of winter.

Fragments of Nature

Aim

* To breakdown images of nature from 'whole' to 'fragments', and use this to inspire and create a work of art.

Materials

* Art Resource Box
* Sketchbooks
* Magnifying glass
* Books and images showing different perspectives on nature
* A collection of found objects such as leaves, small branches, shells, stones and feathers.

Method

Ask group members to look at the found objects very closely, with the naked eye and with the magnifying glass. Encourage them to observe the patterns and textures found on the feathers, tree barks, leaves or rocks, and to have a go at drawing or making rubbings of these. They may like to create abstract work inspired by the patterns they can see when looking closely at the found objects. Suggest that the group photocopies some of the patterns drawn, enlarging or reducing the sizes to see what happens. Suggest that they create abstract images from these copies, if desired. Decide together on how to display completed work.

Alternatives

1 Look at other aspects of nature with group members – for example, scales on a fish can be drawn repeatedly to create patterns and textures. Also consider shapes on horizons, trees, mountains and buildings against the skyline: these can create lines and patterns to trace or copy.

2 Encourage group members to break open rocks, fruit, vegetables or seeds to observe and draw the patterns inside.

Comments

This project offers an ideal opportunity for group members to use their observation skills, and to consider nature from unusual perspectives. Encourage people to remain observant on a daily basis, and use a sketchbook to record observations.

Aim

* **To create calendars using images inspired by 'The Four Seasons'.**

Materials

* **Art Resource Box**
* **White and coloured A4 cards**
* **Hole punch**
* **String or treasury tags**
* **Samples of calendars, with photographs showing pictures of the seasons**
* **Pictures from previous sessions, made and selected by group members.**

Method

Calendars can be created and bound in many different ways. One way is to hold together 13 A4 cards, hole-punched at the top, with string or treasury tags. Make a template or cardboard frame for group members to place over their selected pieces of work, and cut out sections from this work of equal sizes for the calendar. Ask people to select 12 of their own pieces of work, three for each season, and use the template to cut out the pictures for their calendar. Suggest they glue the pictures on to the A4 cards. They can then add the monthly dates on each card, writing these by hand or printing them from a computer. Suggest that they use the thirteenth card for the front of the calendar, and design a cover.

Alternatives

1 Suggest that the group creates an abstract calendar, using colours and shapes inspired by the seasons.

2 This session provides an opportunity for group members to make personal calendars, using photographs, poems of people's experiences and memories connected with each season.

Comments

This project can be done over a year. Drawings, paintings and photographs can be created over the year as the seasons evolve. Use the written word, poems or quotations to complement the images.

The Local Community

In the past, many adults with special needs found themselves participating in art projects confined by four walls, especially if they needed additional support or equipment. These days, more artists with disabilities are able to access activities and events within their local community. There is still a long way to go, not only in terms of access and resources, but also in the wider world's attitude and commitment towards people with a disability leading ordinary lives in the community.

Project 2 looks at some facilities local artists may use to gain inspiration, knowledge and ideas to enhance their work. It is obviously a good idea to check facilities first, before visiting with the group, to ensure access and personal needs can be catered for, and to avoid disappointment and frustrations!

Aims

* **To use a local community resource and setting for an art-based activity**
* **To use the library to inspire and inform art practices within the group**
* **To encourage and develop motivation and informal research skills within the group**
* **To enable group members to make choices, and explore their own perceptions and preferences concerning art.**

Materials

* **A local library and library cards**
* **Transport (if this is necessary to enable some group members to visit the library)**
* **Strong bags to carry books**

Method

Plan and arrange a visit to the local library with the group. In the library, encourage people to browse in all areas, not just the art section – some children's books have very inspiring illustrations! Ask them to select a book (or books), which contains images that appeal to, or inspire, them in any way. Offer support and encouragement where possible.

If some people are unable to choose, ask other group members to make selections for them, showing them the books and images chosen, and saying why they chose those specific books. Encourage people to talk about their choices, and share opinions on the illustrations in the books chosen. Select a variety of books with the group, to borrow for use in future art sessions. Remember to return them on time!

This project can span several weeks or months. Discussion or art appreciation sessions can be held using books selected from the library as a starting point. Encourage people to look at the illustrations that they were drawn to, and to try to explain their choices. Would they like to create images in that style? How would they go about doing this? Hold a practical session in the workspace the following week to enable the group to have a go at re-creating the images they were drawn to. Encourage a fun, non-judgemental environment: each work is not intended to be an exact replica of the original – an individual interpretation of the original style is the ultimate aim!

Using the Local Library as a Resource (cont'd)

Alternatives

1 Select themes with the group before visiting the library. Agree to look for books on specific artists, styles, periods, genres (such as portraiture), or colours. If permitted, work in the library setting: encourage people to make notes and sketches from the books while there.

2 Encourage people to use the library for further inspiration, such as designing book, CD or tape covers, based on the items borrowed. Design a poster advertising an event or new book at the library. See if the library will allow the group to hold a mini exhibition there, or help with one that is planned by the library for the public.

Comments

If people are unable to visit the library, select books on their behalf or check if there is a mobile library service available. Use other resources apart from books to inspire and inform further activities: music tapes, videos, computers/internet services and photocopying machines, can be useful and cost effective – resources, not always available in the workplace or home. Most libraries will order specific books or information not in stock, at the request of browsers.

Aims

* **To offer opportunities for visiting local galleries and exhibitions, to inspire and further motivate the group**
* **To encourage people to record and note observations, new learning and inspirations evoked by these visits.**

Materials

* **Information about local exhibitions and galleries, such as: opening hours, disabled facilities, refreshments, talks and any additional support available**
* **Transport as required**
* **Sketchbooks and drawing tools**
* **Mini tape recorder (optional).**

Method

Select a place to visit, and plan the outing with the group. Before the visit, discuss what people hope to gain from the experience, and encourage them to bring a sketchbook or notebook. If drawing or writing is difficult for some, try using a mini tape recorder to enable them to make a verbal record of the visit. Other group members can use their sketchbooks to record observations and thoughts. An informal discussion can be held with the group over refreshments at the gallery itself, or at your next group session. Ask people to consider what their favourite picture or sculptor was, and why. What did they think of the exhibition itself? Encourage discussion, and consider the way in which the work was presented, and the gallery space used. What inspired or motivated them?

Alternatives

Make a note of the artists people liked or were drawn to, for further research and discussions at a future session.

Comments

Check if any of the local galleries hold open exhibitions for local artists, in which group members could exhibit, if desired, as individuals or collectively.

Visiting Local Places for Inspiration

Aims

* **To offer opportunities for group members to discover and visit places in their local community that will benefit, influence and further inspire their artwork**
* **To practise observation skills, and create a communal sketchbook from these visits.**

Materials

* **Information on local places of interest, such as videos, leaflets or articles on gardens, historic houses, National Trust properties, conservation areas, scenic spots, churches, cathedrals and interesting towns or villages**
* **Sketchbooks and drawing implements.**
* **Mini voice tape recorder (optional).**

Method

Discuss the intended visit with the group, and agree on a destination. Once there, encourage people to have a good look around and use sketchbooks to record anything that 'catches the eye'. They can describe with words as well as images, or use a mini tape recorder. Find time for the group to sit together, to discuss the experience and note any ideas and inspirations that arise from this visit, for future sessions and artwork. For example, they could build a communal sketchbook at the next session: each person could offer work from their own sketchbook to create this larger book.

Alternatives

1 Look out for art weeks when local artists open their homes and studios to the public, and exhibit their work. Art markets are also interesting. Both can be very exciting, motivating and inspiring experiences for the amateur artist.

2 Visit cafés, pubs and restaurants that exhibit work, and enjoy the art, refreshments, and congenial settings!

Comments

Keep a logbook of places visited with groups, and the benefits gained from these visits, for evaluation and future reference.

Aim

* **To paint/draw in open spaces, and enjoy the experience of creating art outdoors.**

Materials

* **Sketchbooks and painting/drawing implements**
* **Lightweight canvas, already stretched (optional)**
* **Lightweight chairs and waterproof mats**
* **Kitchen rolls, gloves, plastic aprons, umbrellas and waterproof clothing**
* **Comfortable layers of clothing – expect to get grubby!**
* **Camera, films, batteries**
* **Refreshments and lots of water!**

Method

Visit a local park, garden or beauty spot, but check facilities such as free parking, wheelchair access and disabled toilets first. When you arrive, find a suitable place for the group to stop and paint or sketch, before you unload the equipment. Allow people to wander off, at a safe distance, to find their own views and space after you have all agreed how long to stay, and where to meet up at the end of the session.

Alternatives

1 Take a camera, and encourage other group members to do the same if possible, so that people can participate in a different way through photography, if they are unable or unwilling to sketch or paint.
2 Suggest that people record the experience with words.

Comments

Some people may be ready to start painting outdoors straight away. Others will be more reserved, and may prefer to observe their companions and enjoy the social interaction. Painting outdoors can be a difficult experience: try not to put pressure on individuals to participate, if they are not in the mood.

Using Other Localities

Aims

* **To look at the ways in which artists use various localities to inspire and influence their work**
* **To encourage group members to research and consider alternative localities.**

Materials

* **Tourist information on local places to visit**
* **Local map/telephone book**
* **Paintings/drawings by other artists, showing a variety of localities.**

Method

Spend time initially with the group, to look at work by other artists. Consider the different places they have used to inspire the main aspect of their picture, or as a background – for example, gardens, studios, dance halls, bars, home interiors, special rooms, trains, boats, by the lake, on the street, on the beach, across the field or in an orchard. Consider some local places that people could visit to make sketches, take photographs or memorise and use for a piece of work: to begin with, this could be someone's back garden, or a local pub. Discuss ideas with group members, decide on a place, and make plans to visit. (Have a contingency plan, with options to choose indoor or outdoor places on the day, if the weather is unpredictable!)

Alternative

Invite group members to bring in a selection of art books, magazines or pictures, which offer ideas and suggestions for interesting localities to paint or draw. These may be pictures by famous artists, or photographs and adverts found in magazines. Encourage the group to discuss why these places could make interesting subjects for a work of art. Hold a practical session to enable people to create their own places, real or fantastic, that are inspired by these images.

Comments

Painting and drawing in public places can be daunting for some artists. If group members are nervous about drawing in public spaces, encourage them to observe only, and make written notes or memorise what they see. They can then work from this when they are back in their usual workspace. With support, practice, and regular visits to places can increase confidence, and eventually, working in public may become an enjoyable, albeit challenging, experience. Find quiet places to begin with.

PART III: THE LOCAL COMMUNITY

Communication

Art is a basic form of communication, used by people through the ages to express ideas, feelings, beliefs and shared perceptions that are real or fantastic. It is an instinctive form of communication that begins spontaneously in childhood, but often appears to dwindle or become constrained as one gets older. The written or verbal word and technology appear to dominate the communication process of adults.

Expectations also appear to change with age, as people are influenced and judged more on how they 'make their mark', in both written and illustrative ways: art tends then to become a chosen activity, career, hobby, or skill/technique to be learned. Yet art is still a natural, powerful and universal communication tool, as well as a therapeutic intervention for children and adults. Many adults who stopped dabbling in art once they left school may well need to begin again in childlike ways, to take up where they left off. Anything goes! Art only needs to be owned and used with conviction, in order for individuals to communicate with confidence, spontaneity and enjoyment, at their own pace and level.

Discussion – 'How Does Art Help Us Communicate?'

Aim

* To explore the power of communication in art, and the ways in which this helps people (including artists) to communicate and share ideas, feelings and messages.

Materials

* A selection of art books, showing the abstract and figurative work of different cultures
* Posters, objects, designs, advertisements and magazines, for discussion.

Method

Encourage group members to look at the pictures, then ask people to select one picture which gives out a 'message', or tells a story – for example, a poster advertising a holiday. Ask questions to stimulate discussion – for example, 'What are the images used in the poster?', 'What is the poster trying to 'say'?' and 'What effect does the image/artwork have on the viewer and why?' Next, using art books, ask them to consider works by well-known artists. What messages do they give to the viewer? How have the artists used art to communicate? Which works do people prefer, and why? Look at traditional and modern art. Compare the differences in terms of communication. What do people notice when they first see an image or artwork? What is the immediate impact?

Alternatives

1 Encourage group members to consider how people communicate in the local community. How do people in the group communicate best? Do they use symbols, signs or the written word? Which do they find the most effective, and why?

2 Offer the group an opportunity to look at other art forms and modes of communication, such as music, dance, drama and digital art.

Comments

Finding new and effective ways to communicate is vitally important to someone with limited communication skills, as well as those who care for them. Art allows people to communicate in diverse and holistic ways, and must never be underestimated as a means of enabling people to explore and develop individualistic and creative communication tools.

This page may be photocopied for instructional use only. *The Art Activity Manual* © Marylyn Cropley 2004

Aim

* **To select a form of visual communication, and use this to send messages within the group.**

Materials

* **Pictures, symbols and photographs that convey a message to the viewer, such as danger signs, weather signs, communication symbols/line drawings, adverts, a painting of a war scene or a hunting trip**
* **Flipchart/large sheet of paper and marker pens (different colours).**

Method

Look through the pictures together, and identify the messages that people think they portray. Consider how the message is presented through the artwork. What did people notice first – the colours, shapes or forms used, or the techniques? Ask volunteers to think of a message that they want to send to the group, and invite them to have a go at drawing the message on the flipchart with the marker pens. The image can be real or abstract. Ask the rest of the group to say what they think the message is, and how it came over from the picture drawn.

It is sometimes difficult to grasp the concept of giving messages, so have examples to assist the group – for example, a set of cards with messages written on them, for people to choose and draw. Have sample line drawings and symbols available, if needed.

Alternatives

1 Make a list of common text messages sent on a mobile phone, such as 'hello', 'meet me at …', 'going to be late', and encourage the group members to illustrate these in humorous ways. Use magazine cuttings and other pictures to inspire and assist people who find it difficult to illustrate from the written word only.

2 Look at examples of modern art. What messages are people getting here? Discuss perceptions with the group. Encourage group members to have a go at creating a piece of modern art with a message – they can do this individually or collectively.

Sending Messages *(cont'd)*

Comments

This activity is an opportunity for facilitators to empower vulnerable artists to explore and find the means to send out messages through art, with confidence and humour. It is important to enable the artists in the group to discover their strengths when communicating through art, and to develop these further – for example, do they use line drawings and symbols? Can they use a computer?

Aims

* **To consider how other artists express feelings and moods through art**
* **To have a go at expressing personal feelings and moods, and to enjoy the experience.**

Materials

* **Art Resource Box**
* **Pictures by artists expressing feelings and moods (atmospheric scenes, or portraits)**
* **Cartoon drawings and photographs of people with different facial expressions.**

Method

Look at the pictures with the group, and discuss how the artists have interpreted moods and feelings in their work. How have they created the atmosphere, or showed people demonstrating different feelings? Ask people to look at the cartoon characters, and to have a go at making faces (or positioning themselves) to imitate some of the feelings/moods portrayed. Suggest that people try drawing each other in the group, while they are making faces to suggest being happy, sad, angry or worried. They can make quick sketches, or take photographs if a camera is available. Encourage people to have a go at drawing cartoon characters, or scenes with people depicting different feelings and moods.

Alternatives

1 Make a list of words describing feelings and moods with the group. Ask them to consider and practise the ways in which these can be expressed in different ways, by using colour, lines, form and different media.
2 Invite people to listen to a variety of music — for example, classical, jazz, pop, and music from other cultures. Encourage them to describe the mood and feelings the music inspires, and to try to capture this on paper.
3 Ask group members to try to re-create, using artwork, an experience or memory that triggers a certain mood or feeling.

Comments

Be prepared to offer support if memories prove to be too traumatic. A supportive, positive atmosphere in the group is essential.

Presenting Thoughts and Ideas

Aims

* **To explore the ways in which thoughts and ideas are presented in art**
* **To present a thought/idea in an art format chosen by the group.**

Materials

* **Art Resource Box**
* **Books, videos and pictures by artists through the ages, depicting an idea or thought. (Include work on modern art, conceptual art, art from other cultures, and images of fashion and design. It is also helpful to have some explanations by the artists on the philosophy behind their work.)**

Method

Look through the resources with the group, and ask someone to select a picture. Ask people to say what they think the image is about. What do they think the artist had in mind when producing the work? Read out any comments by the artist about their work, the concept, or the ideas they were trying to portray. Were they successful in doing this? Encourage discussion in the group. Invite the group to consider the ways in which artists portray concepts and ideas through their work, and to have a go at illustrating an idea themselves. For example, ask the group to do one of the following: design a new mode of transport for artists with a disability; draw an ideal art studio, create abstract images of tomorrow's world and future inventions; illustrate the meaning of life, or a light bulb – the list is endless!

Alternative

Ideas and thoughts pass us by frequently and speedily: somewhere there is a gem that can inspire a powerful piece of artwork. Hold a session to introduce the topic and to enable group members to start a sketchbook – agree to keep this nearby to record any sudden thought or idea that can be expressed through art. These ideas can be developed into a completed piece of artwork later.

Comments

It may be difficult for some people to translate ideas into art forms, especially if working on their own. Encourage people to work together in pairs or smaller groups. This can lighten the load, seem less threatening, and create a fun atmosphere.

Aims

* **To explore the use of symbols and images in communication and art**
* **To enable group members to identify techniques and media which allow them to say what they want, in art form.**

Materials

* **Art Resource Box**
* **Selection of symbols, line drawings and communication symbols, used in everyday life and for people with special needs – for example, symbols depicting everyday objects and food**
* **Flash cards with the written word describing each symbol/object chosen.**

Method

Look at the images and written words selected as a group, and discuss the use of signs and symbols in everyday life. Encourage group members to compare the effectiveness of line drawings and symbols to the written word. Which do people feel has the most impact, and is easier to use and comprehend? Suggest that people have a go at drawing symbols and creating line drawings to convey a written word or statement. Do this by asking people to select a list of everyday objects from the resources available, such as the symbols for table, chair, cup or apple. Then ask people to write out statements saying what they want – for example, 'Please give me the apple', 'I want to sit on the chair'. They can also make up their own statements to say what they want. Encourage group members to try drawing the object or sentences written, and to try to understand each other's messages. Have sample drawings for people to trace or copy if they are unable to draw independently, or ask others in the team to help out.

Alternative

Encourage group members to draw symbols in the air, or mime/sign the word and messages. Use the words verbally alongside the mime or symbol, unless you decide to play a guessing game.

Comments

Repeat this activity frequently: practice makes perfect. Encourage people to think of other ways to use drawing to say what they want.

Telling a Story

Aim

* **To use art to 'tell a story', and to develop further the creative/communication skills of group members.**

Materials

* **Art Resource Box**
* **Large sheet of paper, BluTack®, and a large board or wall space on which to display the paper**
* **Examples of story books with illustrations.**

Method

Look through the books and illustrations with the group. Ask people to consider the ways in which the illustrations portray the story. How is it done? What techniques and media has the artist used? What makes the work effective as an illustration? Suggesting titles to inspire them, ask the group to make up their own short story, with one group member acting as a scribe. Next, ask group members to draw the story together on the large sheet of paper. One person may start, and the others take it in turns to add the picture, or they can gather round and spontaneously draw/paint together on the one sheet. Make sure each person has had the opportunity to make a mark and encourage the group to refer to the story from time to time. Alternatively, someone can volunteer to read the story out slowly as people draw. Then everyone can sit back and enjoy the illustration, while the whole story is read out once again!

Alternatives

1. Create a book of short stories or poems, with illustrations, as a group.
2. A new project can be developed for a group, on researching and exploring the world of illustrations, printing and bookmaking. Visit local illustrators or invite them to give a talk about their work.
3. Do puppet shows with people who are feeling more confident and creative.

Comments

This group exercise can be hilarious for all concerned. Allow people to be as bizarre or serious as they want: the activity can be an uninhibited and confidence-building experience.

Aims

* To look at the ways in which artists through the ages have portrayed the character of a person
* To describe and create a character, and to portray this person in any art form.

Materials

* Art Resource Box
* Portraits and photographs of people by other artists – have a collection of portraits that includes samples of images made through the ages.

Method

Look at the portraits in the collection together. Ask people to select a person that appeals to them from the portraits, and to describe what they actually see – for example, the shape of the face, colour and style of hair, nose, eyes and their clothes. Also ask them to describe the expression on the face, the posture, and any unusual qualities seen. Then invite them to describe other aspects of the person that are not visible, such as the personality of the figure. Suggest that they have a guess at this, and ask why they used the words they did. What has the artist done to give this impression?

Ask people to think about someone they know or see regularly – it could be a relative, the milkman, the postman, a shopkeeper or a stranger on the street. Encourage them to describe how the person looks (in as much detail as possible), their character, and anything else they noticed about them. They can then write a list of words used to describe this person, for reference. Suggest that they draw or paint this character. They can create real or abstract images. Encourage people to use a variety of media, including collage.

Alternatives

1 Use photographs of people who are known to, or are part of, the group.
2 Invite group members to do portraits of each other. Suggest that people start by drawing back views of each other: this can be easier, more fun, and less threatening than beginning with faces.
3 Encourage people to visit local places, to sketch passers-by, or people in pubs and cafés.
4 Start a portrait sketchbook with group members.

Describing a Character *(cont'd)*

Comments

Some people may feel intimidated by this exercise at first. Add some fun to the session by introducing cartoon characters, and suggest people trace or copy these characters. They can then say who they think the cartoons resemble, from people they know. Emphasise that the drawings do not have to be perfect, or look exactly like the person they are portraying.

Aim

* **To design a card or postcard that will communicate a message chosen an individual or the whole group.**

Materials

* **Art Resource Box**
* **A collection of cards/postcards old and new, showing different subjects either in drawings or photographs**
* **Blank postcards and A4 card, white/pastel shades.**

Method

Spread the cards and postcards out on a large table. Ask the group members to look at the cards, and encourage general discussion about what they see. Prompt the group to speak out and share their views on why cards and postcards are used and still popular today. What do people look for when they select a card or postcard? Ask them to think of a person that they would like to send a card to, and why. What would the occasion be? Is it a birthday, anniversary, holiday, or just to say 'hello'? Ask them to design a card for that person, using media of their choice. They can make designs on a blank postcard, or an A4 card folded in half to make a greetings card. Invite people to share the outcome within the group, and actually send their cards if desired!

Alternative

Suggest that group members design postcards or cards for each other, as a safe option or starting point.

Comments

This may be a project people want to develop further and make commercially viable. Find out how skills can be developed to make and sell work commercially. What outlets are there for artists (individually or collectively) to show or sell their cards and postcards?

Speechmark

Creating a Poster

Aims

* **To consider how posters and art influence people in their everyday lives**
* **To design a poster, or portray a message, in a specific style.**

Materials

* **Art Resource Box**
* **Samples of posters promoting a person or product**
* **Books on advertising and poster-making**
* **A3 paper and card**

Method

Ask the group to look at the collection of posters, and have a general discussion on what is being advertised. What are the adverts trying to say to the viewer? How are the posters put together? How are the images, words and language used, together with the composition and media? Select a poster that appeals to the majority of the group, and identify what people liked about the poster and its style. Invite the group to design their own poster. Ask them to decide on the subject-matter (such as a favourite music band, event or product) and, when designing the poster, to consider the composition, colours, words and techniques they will use. They can work individually or in pairs/smaller groups to create the poster, on A3 paper or card. When all have finished, observe the differences in the posters with a similar message.

Alternative

Take group members to visit local places, to see how posters are used and designed – local music shops, book shops, cinemas and theatres are good places to start.

Comments

Use everyday experiences to inspire and influence the group when making posters and finding outlets. Raise issues and frustrations that concern group members on posters. Celebrate an event or personal achievement by creating a poster.

Understanding Self

Achieving a sound understanding of 'self' is difficult, when that very self is continually evolving, influenced by the environment, other people and life experiences. Responses to others, and to life in general, tend to be reactive, habitual and spontaneous. What is truly wanted is not always obtained, and there have to be frequent changes in order to meet individuals' own needs and desires while they are adapting to external changes and pressures.

This conflict is particularly acute in many people with disabilities, who may be dependent on others, and struggle with a sense of identity or self-esteem: they sometimes feel confused, and are torn between meeting their own needs and those of their carers and support services. The situation has improved over the years, and for many vulnerable artists the use of art therapy and art as a form of expression has effectively enabled a development of self-understanding and discovery, locating the 'artist within' through a person-centred approach.

Self-portrait

Aims

* **To gain an awareness of the ways in which artists have interpreted self-image**
* **To develop a positive sense of identity through self-portraiture.**

Materials

* **Art Resource Box**
* **Self-portraits painted by other artists – these can be realistic or abstract, and should include photographs, caricatures and creative writing.**

Method

Spend time allowing the group to look at the work of selected artists and their self-portraits. Start a discussion about the ways in which other artists and photographers have portrayed themselves. Identify styles that individuals find effective and positive, and prompt people to explain their ideas. Invite members to draw or paint a self-portrait. Suggest that they begin by writing a descriptive list of themselves – for example, what they think are their notable physical features, and any other details as desired. Encourage group members to assist each other, if this seems helpful, and to value and respect each person's privacy and dignity. Ask individuals to decide on a style and medium with which they are comfortable. Reassure everyone that portraits do not have to be a close likeness: they can be abstract or figurative. Encourage people to experiment with different media, including collage.

Alternatives

1 Enable group members to use photographs, mirrors or any other reflective surfaces, if they feel comfortable doing this.
2 Group members could create self-caricatures, silhouettes or shadow images.
3 Try abstract portraits, using fingerprints or self-descriptive colours.
4 See if people are bold enough to re-create themselves in different roles.
5 Ask people to draw the back of each other's heads to begin with. This is a popular drawing angle, for any aspiring but vulnerable artist!

Comments

Be aware that people may find this exercise uncomfortable. Allow individuals to watch, or find alternative ways for them to make a self-portrait comfortably.

Speechmark

Aims

* **To look at various works of art, and consider the ways in which relationships between people are presented**
* **To consider personal relationships, and create images of self and others to gain a sense of understanding, self-worth and belonging.**

Materials

* **Art Resource Box**
* **Work by artists and photographers presenting themselves with other people, such as close relatives, friends or casual acquaintances**
* **Photographs of group members with other people, in different situations.**

Method

Look at the work collected by the group, and discuss the portrayal of 'self ' and 'other'. How do artists portray themselves with others? How real, abstract or fantastic are the images, and what impact do they have on the viewer? Do the images portray a level of intimacy or distance between people? How does the artist represent this? Ask the group to think about the people they meet or see everyday: what are their relationships with these people? Are they close, as relatives or friends, or complete strangers (the shopkeeper, bus driver or doctor)? Encourage people to create images of themselves with others in any way they choose. They can use the photographs for reference. Enable individuals to photocopy photographs to make collages, where possible.

Alternative

Encourage and enable the group to research and study famous artists who have produced a variety of artwork that portrays their relationships with others. See if anyone in the group has a favourite artist, and would like to be influenced by this artist when creating their own pictures.

Comments

Some people may need assistance and support to bring in photographs or to ask carers to part with precious pictures. Ask for photocopies instead, if this helps. Invite people to share their final picture, and talk about the relationships they chose, and why.

Lifestyle Portrayed

Aims

* To look at the ways in which other artists portray lifestyles.
* To consider group members' own lifestyles and choose media/techniques to create an image that demonstrates aspects of these lifestyles.

Materials

* Art Resource Box
* Pictures and photographs of people doing different activities within work, leisure, home life, social life and training
* Photographs of group members doing different activities
* A large sheet of paper or card.

Method

Start the session with a general discussion on lifestyles. What kind of lifestyle do people have, in terms of work, leisure, training and relaxation? Ask people to think about what they do on a daily basis, or what they would like to be doing, now or in the near future. Ask individuals in the group to select one activity each, and take it in turns to draw this on the paper. Start to create a collective impression of the different activities and lifestyles within the group. Cut out pictures to stick on for people unable or unwilling to draw. Offer the opportunity for people to then create similar, but individual, lifestyle pictures.

Alternatives

1   Offer an opportunity for individuals to begin a lifestyle diary, in the form of a daily sketchbook. Ask people to use this sketchbook on a daily basis, to illustrate with drawings what they have done.

2   When feeling confident, they can then draw what they hope to do the next day, and develop a 'tomorrow' planner.

Comments

Often people accept current lifestyles as ongoing, and do not consider, or find it hard to think about, change. This is an opportunity for people to imagine and paint themselves in a different lifestyle, as real or unreal as they want, and the activity encourages an imaginative and individual approach to considering life changes and personal development.

Speechmark

Aim

* **To identify, and re-create in art form, something precious to self, choosing suitable media to do this.**

Materials

* **Art Resource Box**
* **A collection of items that group members consider precious – for example, photographs, jewellery, ornaments, items of clothing or special gifts.**

Method

Allow each member of the group to describe and talk about the item they have brought in. What does it look like? Why is it precious to them? Encourage those who have not brought in items to talk about, and try to describe from memory, something precious to them. Ask people to draw or portray the item in a medium of their choice. It can be real or abstract. Involve the group in deciding how the work will be displayed or stored when completed.

Alternatives

1 Instead of objects, consider moments in life, or people that are precious to individuals. Ask the group to try using their thoughts to inspire a drawing or painting.

2 Begin a shared sketchbook or collection of work, or start a 'treasure box' to hold artwork of precious possessions, people, places or moments, belonging to the group. This exercise can help to remind people of positive aspects in their lives, and to store these thoughts for reference when times are difficult.

3 Encourage individuals to write a short poem about a precious object, and to illustrate it.

Comments

Many people tend to hoard things: this exercise can be a comfort to those going through an exceptionally materialistic phase in their lives, and will help them to identify the special treasures hidden amongst the clutter.

Portraying Self in Action

Aims

* **To enable group members to look at and identify images portraying people in action**
* **To encourage group members to consider activities that people engage in on a daily basis, and to select an idea that portrays 'self in action' as inspiration for an artwork.**

Materials

* **Art Resource Box**
* **Pictures, photographs and symbols showing people in action.**

Method

Invite the group to study the pictures together, and discuss how the artist or photographer has captured movement or hinted at action. Where possible, using each other as willing models, ask people to draw quick, spontaneous sketches of each other doing different things – for example, waving, sitting, standing or clapping. Members can also use the pictures and photographs to prompt and inspire. Ask each person to select an activity they do on a regular basis, or one they enjoy or would like to do. Encourage them to create a self-portrait of themselves in action, real or abstract.

Alternatives

1 Some interesting work can be achieved by asking people to use only lines and colours to hint at movement.
2 Suggest that people have a go at copying/ tracing photographs of people and movement as a practice activity.

Comments

Creating movement in art can be very difficult! Encourage people to work quickly and spontaneously, to capture the essence of movement, and not worry about the details. Practise frequently, and work in abstract styles to begin with.

Aims

* **To consider places that matter to people in the group, and to identify a favourite place**
* **To paint or describe the chosen place in art form.**

Materials

* **Art Resource Box**
* **Pictures and photographs of favourite places (if available).**

Method

Begin with a general discussion on favourite places. Encourage people to describe their favourite places, with as much detail as possible, and to explain why they are special to them. Invite them to create this place in art form, using any media they choose. If they want to display the work when it is finished, decide how to do this, individually or collectively.

Alternatives

1 If possible, visit some of the places identified by the group, and work from there, making sketches and taking photographs for reference.
2 Encourage people to develop sketchbooks and keep notes of favourite places, and to re-create these at different times of the day or year.
3 Ask individuals to design a fantasy/favourite place, or a futuristic place, and share the outcome with other group members.
4 Suggest that group members try drawing someone else's favourite place, as that person is describing it verbally. It is fun to do this in pairs or as a group.

Comments

One person's favourite place may be another person's nightmare. Be aware that some sensitive issues may arise for individuals during this discussion. Encourage group members to be sensitive and supportive, in a non-discriminatory way.

Creating a Visual Diary

Aims

✳ **To use art on a daily basis, when making notes in a personal diary**
✳ **To practise basic literacy skills, using line drawings/symbols and the written word in the diary.**

Materials

✳ **Art Resource Box**
✳ **A4 or A5 diaries or sketchbooks.**

Method

Discuss with the group the value of keeping a daily diary or record of daily events, thoughts and experiences. Identify what to keep in a diary, such as appointments, reminders, 'to-do' lists, or personal thoughts on the day's events. Decide with each person how they will use their diary, and what communication tools work best for them. Some may wish to draw freehand and write words, while others may need to copy or trace symbols/line drawings they are familiar with, and have someone else to write the words for them to copy or paste into the diary.

Encourage group members to identify someone they see on a regular basis who could help them to maintain the diary when needed. Begin the diary by marking in special dates/events, such as a relative's birthday. Encourage people to draw a quick sketch of that person on the birth date in the diary – add cake and candles if desired! They can then write the person's name next to the image if desired. Suggest that people add other dates and reminders to their diary in a similar way, and consider how they will use the diary consistently, on a daily basis.

Alternative

Group members can use line drawings, symbols or matchstick people, and trace over carbon paper if they find it difficult to draw freehand. Alternatively, they can cut out and stick in photographs and pictures.

Comments

Encourage people to use the diary on a regular basis, almost like a sketchbook. Offer them a five/ten-minute slot in the weekly sessions to maintain support and commitment.

Aims

* **To enable group members to develop a self-profile, by collecting and collating previous artwork that best describes aspects of themselves**
* **To build a sense of self, and develop self-awareness and confidence.**

Materials

* **Art Resource Box**
* **A4 ring binder files and clear plastic sleeves for each person**
* **A4 card or paper**
* **Collection of work completed by group members.**

Method

Begin by asking each person to look through, and start sorting, any previous artwork they have kept with them. Ask people to select work that describes them in some way, or pieces that they particularly like – for example, 'self in action', 'a favourite place' or a piece of work they are proud of or happy with. Where possible, keep work to A4 size by cutting it down or reducing it, then place it in the clear plastic sleeves. Gradually enable people to build a profile of work they have completed, and which best describes them in some way. They can paste these pieces on to A4 card, add written captions or comments if desired, or leave as pictures only and place in a ring binder to start a personal portfolio.

Alternatives

1 Suggest that people create work on A4 paper or card, specifically for the profile.
2 Encourage people to collect ideas and inspirations for their profiles.
3 People can use words, collage or other media to describe experiences they have had, or a thought or impression of themselves.

Comments

This is an ongoing project, which needs to be done at the individual's own pace, and 'completed' when they say it is!

Art and the Five Senses

Our five senses (sight, smell, taste, hearing and touch) provide a rich source of sensation, stimulation and inspiration. Art incorporates the use of all these senses in diverse ways. Raising awareness of the ways in which we use our senses in art can open doors to new and imaginative ideas. As adults, we hold memories of a range of experiences through our senses, which can be used as a source of inspiration. This is no different for adults with disabilities, who may only need support and encouragement to make future use of these senses, to enhance their artwork and their appreciation of art itself.

Aims

* **To encourage use of sight and observation; to look at and appreciate the environment**
* **To identify art that is visually pleasing, and explore the impact this has on the viewer.**

Materials

* **Information on local places and exhibitions that offer opportunities for visual stimulation and use of observation skills – for example, art galleries, art and craft shops, local events, shop windows, graffiti on walls, a beautiful landscape or building.**

Method

Arrange a visit for the group to a local place of interest, such as an art gallery. Allow time for people to wander around and observe the work on display. Invite people to make a note of an image that has had an impact on them, for any reason, as they wander around. It could be a painting, sculpture, or a person sitting in the café. Encourage people to observe more closely, and to try to identify why something has had a visual impact on them. As you walk around the gallery, encourage the group to say what it is that draws their attention to a painting or sculpture, visually. Is it the subject, colours, shape or form? Ask people to write down, or keep a record yourself of, items selected by the group, and their reasons for their choices. With the information collected from the group, try to identify the aspects that had the most visual impact on people – for example, the use of colours, the size of the image, or the subject-matter. Encourage further discussion over a cup of tea at the gallery, or at another session.

Alternatives

1 Visit other places in the local community – walking around a shopping area can offer a wider diversity of visual stimulation, encourage close observation, and provide discussion points.

2 Shop window displays are good places to look for visual impact and attraction. Give points to different shops on merit for aesthetic, artistic and visual impact.

3 Encourage people to learn from observation, and to create their own image or display that has a visual impact.

Visual Images *(cont'd)*

Comments

Encourage group members to be aware of, and sensitive to, the needs of others in the group who have a visual impairment, without being patronising. Involve visually impaired members in the discussions (if this is what they want!), and help them to see what others see by describing pictures and sculptures in great detail, and in tactile ways. Encourage them to join in and describe what they see or think about the experience.

Aim

* **To explore the use of smell and touch in artwork, and create a tactile, scented picture.**

Materials

* **Tactile fabrics and other materials, such as tissue paper and wads of cotton wool**
* **Lavender oils or dried flowers**
* **Large sheets of card or hardboard.**

Method

Encourage a general discussion about group members' experiences of using smell and touch with art. Invite people to draw a doodle or patterns on the large sheet of card or hardboard, and stick small wads of cotton wool in some of the shapes drawn. These areas are then covered with fabric or paper, using PVA glue. Create other textured surfaces on the board using other materials, and cover with thick paint. Sprinkle two or three drops of the lavender oil on to the padded areas – use sparingly! When it is dry, enjoy the final textured and scented image.

Alternatives

1 Invite the group to arrange a selection of fresh fruit, such as cut up bananas, oranges, apples and strawberries, on plates to create colourful and aromatic patterns and textures. This will appeal to visual, tactile and taste senses! Introduce fresh herbs and spices, in the same way as the fruit, to create patterns and shapes.

2 Suggest making interesting, colourful pizzas, or decorate cakes to stimulate touch, smell, taste and visual senses.

Comments

Exercise caution when using essential oils! Lavender is said to be the most common and safe oil to use, but read the instructions first, and check that no one in the group is pregnant, or adversely affected by the oils.

Sounds and Images

Aim

* **To gain some awareness of the influences of sound and images, when used in art.**

Materials

* **Art Resource Box**
* **A selection of tapes offering a variety of music and sounds as well as a tape recorder.**

Method

Lay out the art materials in advance and play the group a selection of music, then allow them to select their own favourites. While listening, encourage the group to draw or paint freely with the materials of their choice. Suggest that they allow the sounds to influence their movements and the colours they choose. When the session is over, ask the group to compare the difference in their work when listening to soft, gentle music, or hard rhythmic sounds. Did the music influence their work? How? Encourage group discussion.

Alternatives

1 Collect recordings of everyday sounds, such as animals, machines, wind or sea. Play the sounds one at a time, and ask people to draw what they think they heard, quickly. They can also use abstract marks to decribe the sound.

2 Invite group members to sit in quiet spots indoors/outdoors and listen. What kinds of images spring to mind when certain sounds are heard? Suggest that they listen for the sounds of birds, water, traffic – or even silence!

3 Choose instruments or objects that make a noise and select a painting or drawing for the group to study. Then ask them to imagine sounds that will go with the picture. Be bold and use a collection of instruments or objects to create sounds to go with the images – for example, drums to create rhythm for an African sunset. Record the sounds/music made, to listen to while the group enjoys the pictures visually.

Comments

Invite group members to bring in their own music or sound effects, as well as suggesting that people also try this exercise at home or outdoors, listening to music, the birds and even traffic at a bus stop. Encourage them to keep a sketchbook of their 'sound' drawings.

Speechmark

Aims

* **To hold a discussion about the ways in which art is used in the world of food, and the ways in which this affects our senses**
* **To create an abstract meal.**

Materials

* **Art Resource Box**
* **White paper plates**
* **Large sheet of card, on which to display plates**
* **Colour pictures of a wide variety of foods.**

Method

Begin the session with a general discussion about the ways in which art is used in conjunction with food. Points for discussion could include the use of food in advertising, the presentation of meals on posters and menus, and the ways in which the colours, textures and shapes of food are used to entice and affect the senses. Are we influenced by the way meals are presented? How much has the subject of food inspired and motivated artists over the years?

Ask each group member to think about a favourite dish or combination of foods. Using the white paper plates and media of their choice, encourage group members to create this dish on the plate. Suggest that they use lines, shapes and colours only. When finished, have them arrange the plates on the rectangle of card to create an abstract dining table.

Alternatives

1 Invite group members to think of, and re-create, scenes where people are having a meal, food is displayed in interesting and colourful ways, or a still life, such as a fruit bowl, is observed. This could be done as a painting, drawing, sculpture or installation.
2 Ask people to create visually exciting menus, or make prints using fruit and vegetables cut in half. Suggest that group members decorate a T-shirt or cushion with patterns taken from their favourite fruit or vegetable.

Comments

Food can be a rich source of inspiration in art. Many artists were inspired by scenes showing people sharing a meal – in a restaurant, round a dining table, having a picnic, or being fed grapes on a couch.

The Artist Within

The activities in this project are designed to encourage people to focus on their own life experiences and artistic abilities, in a non-judgemental way. Trying to learn a specific technique or style, when you do not want to learn or lack confidence, can be frustrating, and can dampen what little enthusiasm is left! This project allows an opportunity to work with such people in an attempt to draw out the unique and individual style of each person. It aims to find the 'artist within', to build confidence, and to promote enjoyment.

Many artists tend to compare themselves with other contemporary or popular artists. There is also an expectation that a 'true' artist is a 'trained' artist. Learning a skill or technique in any field of life can help to enhance the work, and offers some measure of control and expertise. For many people who say they 'cannot draw or paint', art can also be learned: many of the 'great' artists had very little formal training, and learnt from experience, other artists, trial and error and lots of practice. Some of those who received training in earlier years, frequently ceased to demonstrate this in later years, and deliberately attempted to retrieve the spontaneity, innocence and simplicity of childlike images in their work, reflecting the mannerisms of primitive art and other early styles. The artist within can answer the question, 'what is art?'

Aim

* **To enable group members to experiment with a variety of media and images.**

Materials

* **Art Resource Box**
* **Some random ideas/inspirations with which to work**
* **Any materials requested by the group, in addition to those from the Art Resource Box.**

Method

Set out materials from the Art Resource Box on a table in the workspace. Invite the group to try out the different media to create a chosen picture, or to 'doodle' patterns and designs at random. Create a non-prescriptive, non-judgemental atmosphere, and enjoy the experience. When everyone has finished, look at the competed work, and ask people to say which media they enjoyed using, and why.

Alternative

Encourage and enable the group to research and study work by other artists that demonstrates spontaneous, simplistic and childlike qualities.

Comments

Try to create a fun and relaxing atmosphere. Play music in the background, and offer help and ideas where needed. For people to make simple marks with different media is sufficient: these can be used later to make abstract collages or mosaic if desired, or a section cut out to stand as a work of art in itself. Remember, anything goes!

Finding and Developing a Personal Style

Aims

* **To study the styles and techniques used by other artists, and appreciate the differences between them**
* **To create a work of art in the individual's own style, and identify what makes it unique and special.**

Materials

* **Art Resource Box**
* **Work by other artists, demonstrating a variety of styles – encourage group members to bring in work where possible.**

Method

Consider work by other artists with the group, and identify the different styles, such as, modern, abstract, figurative, impressionist, surreal, brightly coloured, large and spontaneous, or delicate and precise. Have an agreed definition on the group's understanding of 'style'. Discuss the value in 'owning' a style and sticking to it. Ask people if they think they have a specific style when they do art, and encourage them to explain what they think that style is. If they think they have not got an individual style, what makes them say this? If people appear to be struggling to identify a personal style, see if members in the group can help find a style in each other's work. Encourage people to have a go at creating different images using a chosen style. Reassure them that this is not compulsory.

Alternatives

1 Invite local artists to speak to the group, and talk about their work and style of working. See if they are prepared to do a demonstration and/or workshop for the group, on the techniques and style they use.
2 Encourage the group to look at the history of fashion and architecture, from which they will gain some insight into the development and diversity of styles.

Comments

Many artists are known because of a specific style; some change styles frequently. It is important to avoid a feeling of frustration or incompetence if someone feels they do not have a specific style. What matters is that each individual finds a medium or way of working that they enjoy and feel confident with, and which inspires an uninhibited desire to be creative.

PART III: THE ARTIST WITHIN

Speechmark

Aim

* **To offer an opportunity for people to paint or draw freely and spontaneously.**

Materials

* **Art Resource Box**
* **Large sheets of paper.**

Method

Invite group members to select any media from the Art Resource Box, and to make as many marks as they can on the sheet of paper, spontaneously and randomly. After 10 or 15 minutes, stop and look at the work. See if any images or patterns emerge from the work, and if people want to keep it or continue to work on it. Invite people to cut out interesting sections from the large sheet, and display. Encourage the group to continue creating their own work, inspired by the random images, shapes, colours and textures.

Alternatives

1 Play background music to create atmosphere, if desired.
2 Use a trigger word or phase to inspire and help. Start the session and call out a word – for example, 'green', 'snakes', or 'circles within circles'.
3 Have fun creating cartoon characters or strange creatures from the doodles and spontaneous images.

Comments

It can be difficult for some artists to be spontaneous, and some people may find this activity difficult at first. Encourage people to do whatever they feel like doing, and hold these sessions frequently (as a warm-up activity), to enable people to be comfortable with each other, and express themselves more freely.

Expressing and Developing an Idea

Aims

* **To explore and observe the use of designs in everyday life, and consider the ways in which this may interpret an idea**
* **To select an 'idea' as a group, and find ways to present it.**

Materials

* **Art Resource Box**
* **A variety of magazines, books and videos showing everyday objects, architecture, rooms, designs and fashion.**

Method

Ask group members to browse through the books and magazines you have collected, and study the designs, ideas, fashions and architecture found in them. As they do this, begin a discussion about the concepts and ideas people are finding in the books and magazines, and identify their preferences. Then ask members to select and agree on an idea that they wish to develop further and create designs for – for example, 'something used in hot weather', such as a fan, swimsuit or sundress. Invite the group to choose any idea that springs to mind under this category, and to create their own designs, individually or collectively. When they have finished, ask people to lay out their designs on a table or floor, and invite people to talk about their work and how they interpreted the idea.

Alternatives

1   Design a dream home, garden or holiday.
2   Invent a gadget.
3   Re-create themes such as 'war and peace', the perfect world', or 'life on Mars'.
4   What will people look like in the future? If aliens exist what would they look like? Ask people to invent an undersea world, create an ideal pet, or design a new way to travel.

Comments

This activity can encourage people to be aware of their daily surroundings, or to use their imagination and be as realistic or as fantastic as they like. Anything can be re-created or designed to suit the individual, from a simple vase, to a bedroom, car or house. Ask each person to consider the skills they used to interpret an idea. Be positive, build confidence, and enjoy.

This page may be photocopied for instructional use only. The Art Activity Manual © Marilyn Cropley 2004

Speechmark

Aim

* **To look at the ways in which other artists are inspired, and to create artwork from personal inspirations.**

Materials

* **Art Resource Box**
* **A collection of pictures, ideas, objects and words to inspire the group.**

Method

Have a general discussion with the group on what inspires people to be creative. Suggest that they consider work by other artists and group members. Encourage people to look at ideas collected (preferably brought in by the group) and ask each person to select something that inspires them. For example, someone may want to draw or paint an object they saw, use colours and patterns inspired by those found on a scarf, or create a portrait of a person or pet that is special to them.

Alternative

Recommend that people keep a sketchbook nearby, as inspiration can strike when we least expect it, and it is wise not to lose the opportunity. Who knows what great work it could lead to?

Comments

It can be difficult to feel inspired or artistic at any given moment. If people do not feel inspired to work in a practical way, use the session to have a general discussion, or to collect thoughts and ideas for the future. Encourage people to identify times when they feel inspired (and when they do not) and recognise why this is.

It is important to stress that inspiration and a desire or ability to create great works does not always come easily to artists, and it is acceptable to feel uncreative or uninspired at times! Some artists may be motivated by commissions or fame, or the urgent need to contribute to an exhibition. In these cases, they cannot always rely purely on inspiration.

Aims

* **To encourage group members to keep and select their work in order to build up a portfolio**
* **To enjoy the process, and identify what makes a portfolio unique to the artist.**

Materials

* **Collection of works by the group**
* **Something in which to store work – for example, A3/A4 clear plastic sleeves and ring binder files, portfolios, bags or boxes, or home-made portfolios constructed from large sheets of card. (See Part II, Session 14C: Storing Work.)**

Method

Ask each person to look through their work, and select the pieces they want to keep in a portfolio. Offer individuals the opportunity to show the group the contents of their portfolio, and to talk about the work and why it was chosen. Have a discussion to identify what is unique to each artist and why. How would each person describe themselves as an artist, based on their portfolios? Maintain this as an ongoing exercise.

Alternative

If certain individuals do not want to keep the bulk of their work and have nowhere to store it, suggest that they take photographs of the work, if they have a camera or if one can be obtained, before they dispose of any special pieces. A digital camera would be ideal. Alternatively, if the work is A3 or smaller, it can be photocopied and stored in files.

Comments

People lacking in confidence, or with preconceived ideas, can find it difficult to call themselves artists, despite the fact they love to paint and draw, and have been doing this for years. They also find it hard to value and respect their work. Building portfolios helps to demonstrate the importance of artwork, and encourages people to treasure and value their achievements. It also helps them to observe and own the progress they have made. By selecting and discarding work, people begin to identify a style and understand their preferences as artists. If someone is having a bad day, it is better not to do this exercise, as precious work can be lost forever! Let them observe to begin with.

Aims

* **To enable individuals to identify their current skills and goals for personal development**
* **To consider where they would like to be in the future, and set time-scales and action plans.**

Materials

* **Portfolios of group members' work (optional)**
* **Some ideas about dates of courses, exhibitions and other interesting events.**

Method

Encourage group support, and invite each person to talk about their work, achievements, personal strengths and why they enjoy art. Have a general discussion to consider possible outcomes and future activities for people in the group – how can they develop their specific skills and interests? Look at classes offered in the community, plan further groups, or invite an artist to run workshops. Offer the opportunity to set goals. What would people like to achieve in three or four months? Advise people to be as specific as possible. Suggest that individuals make a simple action plan to enable a step-by-step approach, and list the resources needed to enable a successful outcome.

Alternatives

1   If it is possible to run further sessions, look at the project ideas which follow in this section, and plan a further 12–15 week block of sessions with the group, incorporating any other learning needs they may have mentioned.
2   If not, suggest that group members use this book themselves to look for ideas which they can try on their own, or when they meet up in smaller groups.

Comments

Assist individuals to keep their plans realistic and simple where possible. Do not set people up to fail! Some plans may take longer than others and some people will need support from relatives and friends/carers to make initial contacts and realise their goals.

Fragments in Art

An artist is frequently encouraged to be 'observant', and to draw or paint 'what is seen'. The whole picture or complete view is interpreted as realistically as possible, or in abstract form. Some artists will make simple, childlike interpretations of what they see: others may look beyond the obvious, and many will create abstract and fantastic interpretations of what they observe. Yet every picture will be made up of parts – 'fragments', brushstrokes, lines and textures. The total picture has many parts that can be taken for granted or undervalued, especially as a source of inspiration, learning curve, or a challenge to the artist or audience. This project encourages people to be even more observant – to look for fragments within the whole picture and to see the picture from different perspectives.

Aim

* **To understand and explore the effect of using small fragments of paper to create a mosaic.**

Materials

* **Art Resource Box**
* **A3/A4 card**
* **Paper of different colours, textures and patterns, cut or torn into small squares or different mosaic shapes**
* **Books/pictures of mosaic work.**

Method

Invite people to look at the pictures showing different examples of mosaic. Discuss how these are made, the materials used, patterns, colours and shapes. Ask the group to draw simple shapes or images on card, using black marker pens to do the outlines. Then fill in the spaces with the small pieces of paper to create the mosaic. Allow this to be done randomly, or encourage people to think about the colours and textures they want to use, and where they will put them in the picture.

Alternatives

1 Offer opportunities to trace shapes on to cards, or use templates, and outline with black permanent marker pens. Advise members to spread the glue on the cards first, then stick on the mosaic pieces using fingers or tweezers.
2 Group members can make their own mosaic shapes by painting or creating textures on paper, and cutting this into small pieces when dry.
3 Cut up unwanted paintings for mosaic shapes.
4 Use other materials to make mosaics, such as self-hardening clay, soft balsa wood, cork or fabrics.

Comments

PVA glue is not only useful for sticking down most types of light material, but can also be used as a varnish to seal any finished work. Where people may have limited manual dexterity, have available some cut up self-adhesive paper, mosaic plastic tiles and mosaic mirrors for them to try, and provide assistance if needed.

Stepping-stones

Aim

* **To select a fragment from a work of art or image, and work this into a whole new picture, using a 'stepping-stone' approach.**

Materials

* **Art Resource Box**
* **Photocopies of an artwork or photographs owned by group members**
* **Large cards.**

Method

Ask group members to select and photocopy an image or photograph owned by someone in the group. They then need to cut out a small section from the picture to show an abstract image or pattern – for example, part of a face, a hand, or patterns on clothes. Next, cut the card into five shapes, ranging from small to large. Make the shapes look like stepping-stones, keeping them all oval, round or irregular: advise group members to use the same shape for all five 'stones'.

Ask the group to paste the cut-out sections of their photographs on to their smallest 'stones'. Ask them to use this image as inspiration, and to develop patterns and doodles on the smallest stone by drawing over and outwards from the pasted image, until the 'stone' is covered. When done, they then paste the smallest stepping-stone on to the next size up and create patterns around this 'stone'. They need to continue this process until each 'stone' has been pasted on to the next, stepping up in size each time, to create a layered, textured, abstract picture.

Alternative

Instead of fitting each shape into another, keep the 'stones' separate, and develop a theme from small to large. Illustrate a sequence of events or patterns on each 'stone' ranging from small to large. Display on the wall or a floor.

Comments

This exercise offers the facilitator the opportunity to encourage creativity and teamwork with the group. It also offers group members an opportunity to try out their sequencing skills, and use their imaginations.

Speechmark

Aim

* **To create a montage, using shapes and fragments from various sources.**

Materials

* **Art Resource Box**
* **Some cards cut into 10cm squares (as many as possible)**
* **Unwanted magazines, fabrics and materials for cutting up.**

Method

Decide on a theme with the group – for example, 'colours', 'textures', 'black and white', 'people', 'animals' or 'landscape'. Encourage the group to make a list of words around the chosen theme, and use the words to inspire and create images on the square cards. They must fill the squares with colours, shapes, textures and images that relate to the chosen theme. They can use paints, collage, line drawings, or any preferred media: invite the group to select materials from the Art Resource Box. Group members can decide if they want to work individually, in pairs or in small teams.

When the squares are completed and dry, ask the group to create a montage by placing them side by side, horizontally and vertically, to form a large square or rectangular display made up of the smaller squares. Suggest that they can re-arrange the squares if needed, until the final display is pleasing to the group. The squares can then be mounted, and displayed on a wall or board to form a montage of colours and textures.

Alternative

Montage can be used to display cut-out sections of work that people no longer want to keep, creating an abstract wall. The overall picture can be random or abstract in appearance, or the squares can make parts of an overall scene or landscape, rather like a jigsaw puzzle.

Comments

This is an opportunity for group members to work creatively and quietly, on their own at first, or in pairs if they chose to, and then to bring their work together as a team to create a larger communal piece of artwork.

Under the Microscope

Aim

* **To take a microscopic look at nature, and other designs and patterns in the environment, to inspire and use in artwork.**

Materials

* **Art Resource Box**
* **Close-up photographs of nature – for example, images of enlarged cells or hair follicles, fish scales, seeds, leaf veins, insects and patterns in peacock feathers.**

Method

Spend some time with the group looking at the pictures. Ask them to observe how patterns, lines and shapes can look different when viewed from close-up or under a microscope. Ask individuals to select their favourite pictures, and then to have a go at re-creating the patterns and lines in these pictures as abstract images. Suggest that people may like to collect patterns in a sketchbook, for use later as designs on T-shirts, cushions and postcards, or to inspire paintings.

Alternatives

1 If possible, use a microscope to enable members to view things from a different perspective, and make a study of colours and patterns.
2 Take the group out with a magnifying glass to look at nature and the environment. Use a camera with a zoom lens, if one is available, to enlarge interesting patterns and textures in plants, rocks and tree trunks.
3 Photocopy and enlarge segments of the group's own photographs.
4 Collect, and encourage group members to collect, interesting images of things seen from a microscopic perspective, and keep these as a source of inspiration for future work.

Comments

Encourage group members to observe their environment more closely. Suggest they keep a notebook to record anything they see from a microscopic perspective as inspiration for future work, or to share with the rest of the group.

A Different Perspective

Aim

* **To explore work by other artists and designers, and discover different ways to present or interpret an observation, concept, or figments of the imagination.**

Materials

* **A collection of art books, videos and magazines that show how artists have used different perspectives in their work – for example, 'looking up', 'looking down', through doorways and windows and in mirrors. Collect work that demonstrates diverse cultural and spiritual dimensions, as well as figurative or abstract pieces.**

Method

Invite the group to browse through the work by different artists, for 10–15 minutes, then encourage them to discuss the ways in which these artists view their subject-matter, the angles they work from, and the ways in which the work is presented. Consider the different perspectives used by artists on similar or different topics. Encourage group members to identify perspectives that do and do not appeal to them, and ask them to explain their choices.

Alternatives

1 Look at pictures from other cultures, religions and belief systems with the group (including fantasy and science fiction). Encourage people to observe closely and discuss the ways in which the same image or thought may be interpreted and illustrated from different viewpoints.

2 Go for a walk with group members, taking a camera with you, and get them to take pictures of anything that catches their eye from different perspectives – for example, looking up, from behind, through bushes, under arches, near or far.

Comments

If possible, give a brief talk, or invite speakers in to give a presentation, on different perspectives in art.

Into Corners

Aim

* **To look beyond the obvious, by exploring hidden sources of inspiration, and to develop observation skills and the imagination.**

Materials

* **Sketchbooks**
* **Places to visit and explore – for example, gardens, woodland areas, parks, coastal areas (with coves and caves), or indoor places, corners of rooms and the workshop (especially messy ones!)**
* **Camera, preferably with zoom lenses and films.**

Method

Ask people to look around the workshop, especially into corners of the room, inside cupboards or under shelves. See what can be found – for example, cobwebs, scrunched up paper in the corner, crumpled paint tubes by the sink, or thick paint on a wooden pallet. Ask group members to create a still life from these findings, and encourage them to have a go at sketching the arrangement and what they can still see in the corners of the room. Encourage people to take photographs, if desired, for reference when developing artwork.

Alternatives

1 Take the group to places of interest that cry out for exploration, and have lots of interesting 'corners'.

2 Encourage people to look around someone's garden (with permission), vegetable plots, building sites and traditional pubs.

3 Visit National Trust properties, gardens or similar: these can be very exciting places in which to explore corners, and observe nature and history.

Comments

This is a good opportunity for group members to just doodle, or practise drawing skills in earnest. The facilitator will also be offering experiences to group members that will enable them to become more observant when looking into corners, and hopefully enable them to develop a sense of adventure, fun and originality in their work.

Fragments into Whole

Aim

* **To develop a complete image from fragments, using mixed media.**

Materials

* **Art Resource Box**
* **Pictures by artists using the technique of pointillism (images made from dots)**
* **Tools to create dots – for example, pencils, paintbrushes, cotton buds, matchsticks or chopsticks.**

Method

Encourage the group to observe how artists have built up whole images by using dots only (pointillism), rather than lines/brushstrokes. Ask them to draw a scene, landscape or simple outline on paper with pencil. They then need to fill in the outlines with dots, using paints and the tools selected, or other media, such as a thick felt-tip pen, chalk or oil pastels. Suggest that they build up colours and tones to create the light, dark and textures in the picture.

Alternatives

1 Suggest that people use corks or round wooden blocks dipped in paint to make large dots.
2 Encourage people to try using short brush strokes – dabbing the paint on quickly with a brush, or using fingertips.
3 Introduce other media, such as dried beans and pulses or paper cut/torn into small pieces. You can also use confetti, the small circles of paper produced by a hole punch, or self-adhesive dots.

Comments

This activity could take some time and may require a lot of patience! As with jigsaw puzzles, some people like to take their time: if so, it is important to ensure that unfinished work is stored in a safe place and protected between sessions.

Abstract Art

Abstract art is an effective way to work with artists who do not want, or feel unable, to interpret ideas and observations realistically. It is reassuring to know that one does not have to be photo-realistic to be considered an artist! There can be an element of fun and challenge when it comes to interpreting ideas and concepts in an abstract way, and in comprehending work by other artists, or merely appreciating what is seen. How a piece of work turns out is (usually) up to the artist, and only the artist may know what the desired outcome is meant to be.

Abstract art allows an artist to explore and challenge observation skills and titillate the imagination. It offers scope for spontaneity, and for individuals to make their mark without constraints and boundaries, unless they choose to impose these on themselves. Many adults who try art for the first time tend to feel frustrated because they cannot interpret what they see literally. Some will need a lot of encouragement and support to persevere and explore the diversity in abstract art, and feel comforted that they can be creative, despite feeling 'unable to draw or paint'.

Aim

* **To explore abstract art, gain some understanding of the concept, and identify personal likes and dislikes concerning abstract art and artists.**

Materials

* **Books, videos and articles on abstract art and artists**
* **Ideas on exhibitions or places to visit where abstract art is displayed.**

Method

Ask the group to look through the work by other artists, and watch any videos on artists and abstract art. Then invite people to select a picture or artist they like or dislike. Talk together briefly about the work or artist chosen, then ask the group to form a definition of abstract art, based on the work studied and the information collected. Plan a trip with the group, to visit a local or national exhibition showing abstract work.

Alternative

Have a general knowledge quiz on abstract art and artists. Make up the quiz yourself, or split the group into two teams, and have each team make up their own questions with which to challenge the other.

Comments

Encourage people to be open and honest about their views on artists and their work. Far too often the 'emperor's new clothes' syndrome prevails, and people tend to say what they think they should, or agree with others because they lack the knowledge and courage to challenge others and voice their own opinion. Encourage group members to challenge where they feel the need, but try to keep it friendly!

Sometimes, people may initially dislike an artist or their work because they have insufficient knowledge or understanding of where the artist is coming from. Some take a picture at face value, and comment on what they see. This is fine if that is how one wishes to appreciate a work of art, but encourage people to widen their knowledge and experience of a specific artist and their work, and see if views change once they have done this.

Speechmark

Working from an Inspirational Abstract Artist

Aim

* **To have the opportunity to produce work inspired by abstract art and artists.**

Materials

* **Art Resource Box**
* **Sketchbooks**
* **Information and pictures on abstract work and artists, preferably selected and brought in by the group.**

Method

Ask each person to look at the information available on abstract art and artists, and to then select an artist that they like or are interested in. Discuss people's choices, and encourage people to talk about the style of the artists chosen, their work, subject-matter, techniques and media used, the impression created, concepts and ideas expressed, and how effective they find the picture. What makes the work an abstract?

Encourage people to begin a sketchbook in which to make notes on the artist chosen, and develop inspiration from their work. Ask them to spend some time working on the sketchbooks, and finish the session with a brief discussion on what people have learned from the experience.

Alternative

If the group is willing, aim towards presenting an exhibition of work by group members, based on inspiration from other artists. Begin with a private group exhibition, and see how many people can recognise the source of inspiration in others' work.

Comments

This project can take several weeks, depending on the level of interest shown by the group. Encourage people to spend time using resources such as the library, websites and art galleries, to collect information on their chosen artist.

Aim

* **To select images from magazines, books, photographs and sketchbooks, and use them to inspire an abstract work of art.**

Materials

* **Art Resource Box**
* **A selection of pictures, photographs, magazines and sketches of different images**
* **Tracing paper, carbon papers, and access to a photocopier.**

Method

Invite the group to select various images that they like from the collection of photographs and magazines. Ask people to copy or trace the outline of the images, or only a fragment of an image, such as part of a shoe or hand. Advise people to outline the shapes only, leaving out details, and avoid re-creating the original image in a realistic way. Suggest that they photocopy parts of an image, and experiment by enlarging or reducing these parts.

When this is done, encourage people to cut up these pictures so that they have a collection of smaller abstract images. They can then glue these images on to paper or card to build an abstract collage, either individually or collectively. When the collage is completed, suggest that they use it to inspire them to create an abstract painting.

Alternative

Hold sessions where group members are encouraged to create large communal abstract works or where people work in pairs, supporting each other.

Comments

Encourage group members to visit their local library or the internet, to find out more about abstract art and collage work, if they are interested and keen to develop this activity further.

Reality into Abstract

Aim

* **To select realistic images from everyday life, and develop these into abstract forms.**

Materials

* **Art Resource Box**
* **A collection of photographs, books and pictures of everyday objects or simple images**
* **Simple objects for a still life, such as plants, a vase, some stones or shells.**

Method

Ask each group member to select a photograph or image of an object, or display a still life on a table. Invite people to sketch the still life or the image they have chosen: they should draw what they see, and be spontaneous and quick. Encourage people to consider lines, shapes and forms and colours only, and to keep working with the image until it no longer looks like the original. Share the completed work, and enjoy the results.

Alternatives

1 The same process can be used for any subject-matter – for example, life drawings, landscape, animals, or any ideas that can be developed in some way. Sketch the subject, quickly and repeatedly, until it develops into an abstract image.
2 Suggest that people try tracing around lines and shapes only, and create abstract images with the tracings.
3 Use photographs. Photocopy and enlarge images until they become distorted, and only a fragment of the original is shown. Use this to inspire members to develop an abstract idea.

Comments

If someone is struggling to go abstract, suggest that they try drawing a simple shape using straight lines only – for example, draw a ball or a fish without using curves!

Spirituality and Culture

Historically, art has played an important role in religion and other spiritual lifestyles and cultures, not only aesthetically or symbolically, but also as a form of communication and interpretation of belief systems and values. It demonstrates the diversity and wonder of human nature, and the importance for humanity to be creative and communicate through art. This is a common ground for all cultures and belief systems. Studying and celebrating art's contribution to religion and culture is helpful to any person interested in art, in order to understand its power and descent through the ages.

Art has the potential to be an effective tool in managing diversity, offering a person-centred approach which assists people to identify a sense of 'self' and a belief system. It speaks in many languages, and is owned by no single person, thus allowing an objective but sensitive way to encourage a non-discriminatory sharing of views and values. The secret is to validate each person and enjoy the shared experiences and artistic achievements that emanate from different cultures, religions and spiritual beliefs.

Discussion – 'Art and Religion'

Aim

* **To explore the ways in which art is used in religion, and to discuss the impact and effectiveness that religious art has on its audience.**

Materials

* **Some books, videos, pictures, statues, symbols or religious objects – for example, rosaries, prayer beads, illustrated bibles, prayer books and small statues.**

Method

Lay out the books and items on a table for all to see, and ask the group members to have a look at them. Invite them to observe, identify and discuss the different art techniques, materials and formats used in different religions, using the items as prompts. Find ways to enable members to look at paintings, statues, decorations, symbolic objects and architecture in different places of worship. Encourage them to enjoy the diversity and beauty of the artwork, and to consider the historic journey art has taken over the years, through different religions.

Alternatives

1 Arrange for groups to visit local places of worship, to admire the way in which art and religion integrate within the local community.
2 Suggest that group members study the use of words and music in religion.

Comments

Keep discussions as objective and non-judgemental as possible. Focus on the artwork emanating from different religions, rather than debating the practices. Be sensitive to religious beliefs within the group. For some people, spirituality is integrated with religion. However, others may not see spirituality as a religion, and some will be atheist or agnostic. Embrace all, and reassure group members that this project is not intended to recruit converts to any particular religion, but to appreciate art in religion. Group leaders must be honest if their own knowledge is inadequate. Keep information factual, or invite religious leaders or representatives to give talks.

Speechmark

Aim

* To explore art and culture, and share different views and observations within the group.

Materials

* Books, photographs, videos, and magazines that portray the use of art in various cultures around the world. Consider lifestyles, appearances, food, language, belief systems, ideas, architecture and fashion.

Method

Collect the information yourself initially (from libraries, travel agencies and similar sources). Look at the information collected with the group, and have a general discussion on the diversity of art within different cultures. How does art compare when looking at styles, materials and formats used? Are artworks in one culture influenced by, or similar to, other cultures? Ask people to consider the different cultural backgrounds within the group. What are group members' preferences, and what do they feel they can learn from other cultures, as well as their own, to enhance and stimulate their work and styles?

Alternatives

1 Ask people to bring in any books, items, clothing or artwork from home that they think best represent their own culture, or one that they admire. Invite them to share this with the group in an informal way, or more formally as a talk or presentation, if desirable.

2 Look out for local or national exhibitions or talks on other cultures and art that the group could visit/attend.

Comments

Focus on this project as an art appreciation exercise. It may be difficult to avoid discriminatory remarks and prejudices within the discussion. If comments appear to treat some cultures or lifestyles less favourably than others, and prejudices lead to discriminatory and hurtful remarks, it is wise to be firm and deal with this as it occurs. Remind group members of the purpose of this project. It is important for people to feel able to voice their likes and dislikes of certain pieces of art, without feeling intimidated.

Expressing Beliefs Visually

Aim

* **To discuss, in general, beliefs and values within the group, and to find ways to demonstrate these visually.**

Materials

* **Art Resource Box**
* **Collection of images, pictures, books and words that express a belief – for example, religious images, spiritual images showing peace, tranquillity, war, peace, fairies, UFOs or heaven!**

Method

Start a general discussion about what people believe in. Use themes if helpful – for example, 'What is the universe like?', 'If other species exist, what would they look like?' and 'What do people think a god/creator would look like?' Write down the words that people use to describe what they believe, or how they perceive the answers to these questions. Ask the group to select some of the words, and have a discussion about the ways in which these words could be expressed visually. Encourage group members to be objective and non-judgemental, and to value beliefs group members have shared. Suggest that they have a go at illustrating some of the beliefs identified, individually or as a group.

Alternatives

1 Encourage people to explore beliefs and spiritual journeys by keeping a visual journal or sketchbook to record thoughts, inspirations and experiences. They can refer to this for spiritual comfort or artistic inspiration, as needed.

2 Encourage people to listen to music and words from different cultures, religions and beliefs. Suggest that they make notes and sketches, and use these as artistic inspiration for future work.

Comments

Enable members to stay focused, and link beliefs highlighted to spirituality and culture. Support individuals to express their beliefs with confidence, and maintain a non-judgemental approach within the group. Allow people to keep their work confidential and private. Try to keep the exercise simple and fun.

Mandalas

Aim

* **To create images and artwork inspired by the basic concept of a mandala. (A mandala is an image within a circle that tells a story, describes a moment, or portrays a concept that is abstract or natural. Circles are common shapes in nature and art. They can be used therapeutically to illustrate a spiritual or cultural theme.)**

Materials

* **Art Resource Box**
* **Large, round plates to use as templates, or compasses to make circles**
* **Information about, and pictures of, mandalas – these can be obtained from libraries, books on alternative therapies or the internet**
* **Pictures of circles, from nature or created artificially – for example, the sun, the centre of a flower, crop circles, jewellery and Celtic symbols.**

Method

Involve the group in doing some research into mandalas (optional). Consider the idea of using circles, inspired by the philosophy behind mandalas. Encourage people to work freely and spontaneously to create images or patterns within circles, the outcome of which will be up to each individual. The final image can be used as a focus for meditation, as a gift to a friend/relative, or displayed in a personal space to further inspire or gain insight into self as an artist and individual.

To create mandalas, ask group members to draw circles of any size on paper, using round templates, or pairs of compasses. Suggest that they sit for a minute or two in a quiet setting, looking at the space within the circle. When ready, ask them to start to draw or paint whatever patterns, shapes and colours come into their minds. Encourage people to be spontaneous and to enjoy the process.

Alternatives

1 Use relaxation tapes, candles and soft lights to create a tranquil atmosphere, and enable group members to make mandalas that can be used for meditation and relaxation.

Mandalas *(cont'd)*

2 Encourage the group to study the ways in which different religions and cultures use mandalas and circles.

3 Suggest that group members consider natural circles, and circles in technology and computers.

Comments

This can be a very therapeutic and inspiring activity for the group, and can range from being simple and objective, to profound, intimate and subjective. Be aware of people's feelings and expectations as they do this exercise. Where someone may feel a little timid to start with, it may be helpful to suggest that they simply doodle, making patterns within circles to see where this takes them.

Aim

* **To create images using colours, shapes and ideas inspired by stained glass windows.**

Materials

* **Pencils**
* **Black permanent marker pens**
* **Felt-tip pens or highlighter pens**
* **Black card, cut to make frames**
* **Tracing paper**
* **Pictures of stained glass**
* **Simple images or photographs, special to group members.**

Method

Invite the group to look at the pictures of stained glass windows, and to explore the use of light, colour, shape, and the purpose of this art form. Are the windows merely decorative, or do they tell a story or impart a specific message? Decide on a theme with the group to inspire the making of a stained glass window – for example, a nativity scene, or an important person/scene in history or in someone's personal life. Use the photographs and pictures brought in by the group.

Ask group members to trace around the images, or draw freehand (with pencil first) on the tracing paper. When satisfied with the image, suggest they go over the outlines with the black marker pen. They can then fill in the shapes with colours, using felt-tip pens or highlighter pens. When finished, they will need to frame the work with the black card frames, and display it on a window, or hang it as a mobile where light can shine through the coloured-in tracing paper.

Alternatives

1   The group could use glass or acrylic paints on glass surfaces and mirrors.
2   Visit churches and buildings to experience the effect of real stained glass.
3   Enable group members to access workshops or activities where they can experience making, or observe others making, real stained glass windows.

Comments

Stained glass windows often have a history, and tell a story. This is an opportunity for people to study the art form in great depth, and to use this technique to communicate their own stories and ideas.

Icons and Panels

Aim

* **To look at religious use of icons and panels over the centuries, and create a panel to tell a story.**

Materials

* **Art Resource Box**
* **Thick card or lightweight wood**
* **Strong tape to bind panels together**
* **Gold paint/gold pens**
* **Varnish or PVA glue.**

Method

Encourage a discussion within the group about the history and use of icons/panels in different cultures and religions. Ask them to consider how each panel tells a story, or portrays a character. Ask the group to think of a modern story or character that they would like to portray. They can then create panels by cutting out rectangles of card or wood, and use the tape to bind and 'hinge' the panels together. Next, they will need to paint over the panels with white acrylic or emulsion paint. Invite people to design, draw and paint images to 'tell a story', on the prepared panels. Suggest that they use the gold paints to give an aged look and a similar effect to the panels and icons seen in pictures/books.

Alternatives

1 Take the group to visit exhibitions or places where panels and icons can be viewed. Encourage people to consider how the objects were made, and use similar materials (such as wood, varnish or gold paint) to give an authentic look to the group's own work.

2 Ask the group members to think about events or people that are important to them, such as celebrations, people they know, family events, or their interpretation of themes such as the four seasons, religious events or world events. Ask how they might interpret these events on icons and panels. Invite them to have a go at carrying out their ideas!

Comments

Find an outlet in the community to enable the group to present their completed work if they want to, or find an inspiring project for them to participate in, such as forthcoming events in the library, school, hospital or a place of worship.

Aim

* **To look at the ways in which art is used in other cultures, and to seek inspiration from the findings.**

Materials

* **Art Resource Box**
* **Sketchbooks**
* **Photographs, books and videos on other cultures and art – include ancient and modern art.**

Method

Encourage the group to explore the use of art throughout history, and in as many different cultures as possible. Encourage people to look at the work collected and select a style and/or culture that is interesting or inspiring to them. Invite them to have a go at creating a piece of work inspired by the images selected. Suggest that they begin a sketchbook, and spend time researching further if necessary.

Alternatives

1 Suggest to the group that they focus on specific elements in art, such as the sculpture, textiles, ceramics, fashion or buildings of different cultures, and create work inspired by one of these.

2 Suggest that people work with themes that affect all cultures, and experiment by creating different images from these. Encourage them to consider how the images might be interpreted in different ways within each culture. Themes might include landscapes, music, use of colour, use of media, patterns, designs and decorative objects.

3 Encourage people to consider cultures within communities, and ones that evolved over time, such as artistic periods in music, or 'movements' such as punk, heavy metal and rap! How are these represented through art? Encourage the group to celebrate the diversity together, and to create work inspired by cultural music.

Comments

Encourage people to continue to research and explore art and other cultures in order to collect ideas and inspirations for future work, or merely to appreciate and enjoy!

Art in Book Form

Art has been used to illustrate the written word for hundreds of years. Books can be a source of inspiration, and can encourage artists to create illustrations or continue their practice at times when motivation seems 'blocked'. For example, using the title of a book can inspire and trigger the imagination to create a picture. Better still, why not make a book? It could be a collection of poems, short stories, words of inspiration, a journal or a biography.

The combination of creative writing and visual images can be a very powerful art form, opening doors for the imagination. Books come in all shapes and sizes, and do not have to end up as published works (although there is no harm in trying!) – it can be fun, challenging, and very rewarding when the final work is put together. Creating books with groups allows scope to develop a range of interpersonal and confidence building skills.

Aim

* To enable the group to value and appreciate the use of sketchbooks, and begin to develop their own sketchbooks.

Materials

* Art Resource Box
* A4 or A5 ring binder files
* Hole punch
* A4 and A3 paper, of different textures and colours
* Examples of completed sketchbooks, begged, borrowed, or bought from artists!

Method

Have a general discussion with the group to begin with, on the purpose and value of using sketchbooks. Ask group members to create a blank sketchbook by filling the ring binder file (any size) with paper. They can cut various types of textured drawing papers to size, and use the hole punch to insert these in the ring binders. Ask each person to consider how they would use their sketchbook, and to decide if it will contain a random collection of sketches, or work from a set theme (such as flowers, animals, people or landscapes). Plan activities together that will enable people to use their sketchbooks consistently. Encourage the group to consider ways to evaluate their use of the sketchbooks regularly, to share outcomes and ideas, and to motivate each other to maintain the sketchbooks.

Alternative

Suggest that people include words, photographs and cuttings from magazines or other sources of information in their sketchbooks, as well as drawings.

Comments

Some artists are disciplined and consistent with sketchbooks, and use the contents inventively to further enhance their work. Others may need support and an external discipline to begin or continue! It can be fun showing sketchbooks to others, and using them to reflect on completed work. Encourage people to keep and value their sketchbooks. Some sketchbooks can be far more exciting and inspiring than the final piece! Ring binder files make it easier to add or remove sketches.

A Book with a Difference

Aim

* **To create 'concertina' books, and use them to display artwork and ideas.**

Materials

* **Art Resource Box**
* **Sheets of card or thick paper**
* **Sample of a concertina book**
* **Ideas and themes for the books.**

Method

Show the group a sample book at the beginning of this session, and invite group members to examine it before making their own versions. Ask them to cut a length of card 75cm long and 15cm wide, and then fold the card at 15cm intervals to create a concertina shape (some people will need help with this). Explain that this will form the basic format for the book. Invite participants to decide on a theme for the book – for example, aspects of nature, colours, patterns and textures, or a sequence of events or designs. Next, suggest that people create images on each section of the book, using any media or technique they wish. They can work directly on to the card/book, or on other materials, which can be cut out later, and pasted on to the card/book. Remind people that they will need to have a front and back to the book. When ready to exhibit the completed work, suggest that people stand the books upright on a flat surface (a table or shelf), or hang them up – lengthways as mobiles, or flat against a wall.

Alternatives

1 Suggest to group members that they can use words alongside images, or materials such as clay, wood and textiles instead of card.
2 Concertina books can also be used to display photographs or collages, and to provide an illustrated booklet for CDs or tapes.

Comments

The concertina style of the book allows for a diversity of materials and topics to be used by the artist. It enables the facilitator to offer a novel way to stimulate the imagination within the group. This is an activity that benefits both the individual artist and those wishing to work together as a small team.

Speechmark

Aim

* **To create books that are tactile as well as visual.**

Materials

* **Art Resource Box**
* **A5 cards**
* **Hole punch**
* **A selection of materials with which to create textured surfaces, such as paper, fabrics, seeds, string, net and leaves**
* **String, shoelaces or cord with which to bind books.**

Method

Encourage the group to decide on a simple topic for a book – for example, birds, flowers, colours and shapes. Ask them to select a few A5 cards, and then punch holes in the sides of the cards, to enable them to be bound together to form the book when completed. Group members then need to cover each card, including the front cover, with materials to create textured surfaces. They can glue items on firmly with PVA glue and leave the work to dry, then varnish over with further layers of PVA glue. Demonstrate how people can bind the cards loosely together, with string or cord of a compatible colour. They will need to ensure that the pages can be turned easily, and may want assistance to do this.

Alternatives

1 Offer the group opportunities to use other material with which to make books, such as clay tiles, balsa wood, textured fabrics and home-made paper.
2 If group members like to sew, use interesting threads and string, or create 'woven' books.

Comments

Textured books can be given as gifts, presented in decorative boxes or 'pouches', or kept for personal use. This is a fun and productive way to work with people who need, or prefer to use, tactile senses to create or communicate. If making books for children or people with sight impairments, make sure there are no sharp edges or small items that can come away when touched. If anyone in the group uses braille, enable them to incorporate this in their work, where possible.

Storytape and Books

Aim

* **To create storytapes and books, and to illustrate these with personal artwork.**

Materials

* **Art Resource Box**
* **A4 ring binder files**
* **Clear sleeves**
* **A4 cards**
* **Blank tapes, tape recorder and microphone.**

Method

Work with participants to create a short story or several poems, individually or as a group. Invite someone to read the story or poems onto the tape – add music and sound effects if desired. Then encourage the group to listen to the tape, and use the words and the imagination to inspire them to create images, abstract or realistic, to go with the book. Suggest that they create the images on A4 paper, and have the text (handwritten or typed on A4 cards) alongside the images. They can present the finished work in clear plastic sleeves in a file to create the book. Suggest that people design a front cover, and help them to attach the tape (in a case) to the inside cover of the file with double-sided tape. Invite them to listen to the tape, while looking through and enjoying the book.

Alternative

Any topic can be chosen, including current issues such as conservation or disability, places of interest and personal expressions, both real and imaginary. This project offers a total communication approach to art and self-expression.

Comments

This project will cater for a diversity of interests and skills within a group, and can be fun as a shared activity.

10

Going Up, Going Down

This section offers ideas for exhibiting group members' work from different perspectives – it is offered as an alternative to framed work and displays on walls. The project looks at using mobiles, sculptures and installations to exhibit artwork completed by the group, as well making use of these as art forms in themselves. It is worthwhile encouraging group members to explore alternative ways to exhibit their work, alongside the traditional forms of exhibition. Visit local and modern galleries for inspiration: observe how work is exhibited and the diverse ways in which artists portray ideas and concepts in art today.

Mobiles

Aim

* **To create mobiles for hanging and displaying work created by group members.**

Materials

* **Art Resource Box**
* **Black cards or thick paper, 10cm x 15cm. Cut out the centres to create frames approximately 1.5cm wide**
* **Drawing paper, to sandwich between the black frames**
* **Hole punch**
* **Large paper-clips**
* **String/wire, PVA glue, double-sided tape**
* **Hooks to attach string/wire to walls if needed**
* **Wire coat hangers (optional).**

Method

Invite group members to create images, abstract or real, on the drawing paper. They can choose a theme to work from, or make random images. They will need to work on both sides of the paper, and sandwich the finished work between two of the black frames, by gluing the edges together or using double-sided tape. Ask them to create several pictures like this.

When the pictures are completed, instruct group members to punch two holes evenly at the top and bottom edges of the frames and to 'thread' two of the large paper-clips through each of the holes. Show people how to link the paper-clips to the other framed images, using the punched holes until they have a row of black frames that will hang as a mobile. They can use string to attach the top two paper clips to a coat hanger. The mobiles can hang freely from string or wire strung across the room, or from a hook in the wall. This display can be used to exhibit silk paintings, or work on tracing paper, such as stained glass effect pictures. It can be any size, so long as the weight can be supported when the mobile is hung.

This page may be photocopied for instructional use only. *The Art Activity Manual* © Marylyn Cropley 2004

Alternatives

1 Suggest that group members try using lightweight cardboard boxes – large, empty cereal boxes work well – as mobiles. They can paint these white or black and attach their artwork to the sides of the boxes. Attach the boxes to each other, or hang separately, to display as a mobile.

2 Have a go at creating a sensory corner installation, by encouraging the group to decorate fabrics or lightweight materials with silk paints, acrylics and fabric dyes. They could also try weaving their own fabrics. They can hang these materials by attaching them to wire stretched across the corner of the room like a clothes-line.

3 Group members can also make mobiles from recycled materials – for example, the polystyrene circles used as pizza bases can be painted with acrylic and cut to form spirals. These make excellent lightweight and colourful mobiles. Use unwanted CDs as well. Encourage people to paint over them with acrylic paint, or cover them with their own drawings and patterns, produced on paper and glued to the CD. Drill holes at edges of the CDs, and hang them up with lightweight wire, or thread string through the centres of the CDs.

4 Paste people's work on to polystyrene squares or light mount boards, and hang them from ceiling using wire 'clothes-lines', to create mobile displays of work.

Comments

These are just a few ideas to suggest to the group for displaying their work. Where possible, encourage individuals to create their own displays and develop their own ideas. Some will need help to present and hang work, and the facilitator may need to do this outside session time – be warned!

Sculptures

Aim

* **To build a sculpture from recycled materials, and use this to display the group's artwork.**

Materials

* **Art Resource Box**
* **Recycled, lightweight, cardboard boxes of different sizes**
* **Emulsion paint or white paper with which to cover boxes**
* **PVA glue.**

Method

Instruct the group to paint the boxes white, or cover them with plain paper. Decide together how to build a structure: this can be done by stacking the boxes on top of each other, or by having some 'protruding' from a central pillar of boxes. Encourage group members to create an abstract sculpture with the boxes, then glue the boxes together when people are happy with the final structure. When the glue is dry, suggest that people can decorate the sides of the boxes by sticking on a selection of artwork they have completed in previous sessions. Alternatively, invite them to create new designs and paint directly on the boxes. They can make textures and patterns using collage material, if desired.

Alternatives

1 Recycle other materials to create structures that can be used to exhibit or hang work. For example, wrap small pieces of work around tin cans, and stack the cans to create an installation.

2 Find a hat stand or a similar object at a car boot sale or charity shop, paint it white or black, and use it to hang mobiles.

3 If they are able to, group members could make their own boxes with card, wood or stuffed fabric, display work on the sides of these, and stack them up to make a sculpture.

4 Use a stack of lightweight wooden boxes or cubes to display a combination of creative writing and images completed in previous sessions.

Comments

Ensure that the boxes are securely attached to each other, and that the glue has dried before people start decorating the sides. This format can be used to exhibit work where wall space is scarce, or to stand in prominent places to share messages and make statements. It may be necessary to have some stacking boxes and plinths made especially for the group: ask a friend, relative or local college if they know any carpenters or students who are prepared to do this just for the practice, experience and fun!

Photographs, Photocopying and Art

Photographs have been taken and used by artists over the years as an alternative to sketchbooks, and as an aid to memory. It can be difficult and frustrating for some people to draw and paint landscapes or portraits, without taking a break from their work, or returning another day. Some artists may find it difficult to sit still for too long because of a disability, and others have limited concentration spans. Although one endeavours to capture the real thing with pencil or brush, changing lights and all, photographs can be an invaluable aid to the artist. As well as a reference, they can also serve as inspiration to re-create and enhance a moment in time, in an abstract or figurative way, long after the moment has passed.

Photocopying a drawing or image can help to identify lines and tones more easily, especially when changing a colour image to black and white. A pencil or charcoal sketch can be preserved in this way, and can still look effective. Copies of black and white original artwork can be used to paint over in different colours and tones, for practice. The use of photographs and photocopies may be influenced by copyright guidelines: this needs to be clarified before you begin, and permission sought, as and where necessary. The work in these projects will be owned and created by the individual artists for personal use; however, if in doubt, check it out!

Aims

* **To take photographs of subjects in which group members are interested, or to collect personal photographs for future use**
* **To select a photograph to photocopy and use in a piece of artwork.**

Materials

* **Art Resource Box**
* **Albums, or similar, in which to store photographs**
* **A camera and film**
* **Group members' photographs of people, places, objects or moments in time**
* **Paper and card.**

Method

Look at the photographs together, and invite individuals to select one or two pictures they would like to use to inspire a piece of artwork. Ask members to try drawing the images in the photograph. They can make it real or abstract, and add colour or textures as desired. Use the camera to take photographs of local places and people, either in advance of sessions, or with group members during sessions. People can photocopy the images, and then use the copies to practise blocking in colours, shades, tones and textures, experimenting with a variety of media.

Alternatives

1   Invite the group to select a theme to photograph, such as 'People I know', 'My pets', 'Where I live', or 'My favourite place'. They can take pictures of the chosen theme over an agreed period of time, and use the results in a session to produce a piece of artwork.

2   Encourage the group to keep their less successful photographs. These can be cut up to create interesting, abstract collages.

Comments

Photographs can be photocopied, and the copies drawn or painted over, or they can be cut out and used as collage, or as a specific image within a painting. Be aware that some people may not own personal photographs, or wish to share those they do own with others, for various reasons. Encourage them to take new pictures if they have a camera, or have some available that have already been taken by group members who are willing to share.

Using Photocopying to Inspire and Create

Aim

* To use photocopies of personal artwork for collage, portfolios, and new images and artworks.

Materials

* Art Resource Box
* Paper or card
* A4 ring binder files and clear plastic sleeves
* A collection of artwork/photographs (A4/A3 or smaller) by group members
* Access to a photocopying machine.

Method

Ask people to bring in a selection of their own work and photographs. Encourage them to identify one or two pieces they like or want to work with. They can then photocopy the work several times – colour copies are expensive, but black and white images can also be very effective. Suggest that they have a go at drawing or painting on the copies, to experiment and develop the artwork further, or cut out the photocopied images to create interesting collages or abstract work.

Alternatives

1 Suggest that group members can enlarge or reduce images they have made, for special effects and collage work.
2 Invite people to try enlarging a small part of an image, and begin an abstract picture inspired by this.
3 Photocopied images of people's original work can be used for decoupage when making calendars or cards.

Comments

People who are reluctant, or feel unable, to draw freehand can practise and gain confidence by drawing or colouring over the lines and spaces of a photocopied image. Artwork can be saved and protected by photocopying in black and white (or colour, if your budget allows), and stored in clear plastic sleeves in a file, for future use and reference.

Speechmark

Art in Boxes

Artworks can be presented and framed in many different ways – boxes can be used as deep frames or containers to display and exhibit finished work, or as an integral part of the work itself. Boxes are also very useful for storing art materials and items for future work and reference. They can be decorated with patterns and designs unique to the artist, and used for gifts, storage or in exhibitions. This project gives a few ideas for groups to explore further!

Boxed Theme – 'A Moment in Time'

Aim

* **To represent 'a moment in time' in a creative way, using boxes as frames.**

Materials

* **Art Resource Box**
* **A collection of box frames, or boxes in which to display work**
* **Pictures or samples of 'art in boxes' by other artists**
* **A collection of items and found objects relevant to the theme chosen for the boxed project.**

Method

Ask the group to spend a minute or two in silence, and to reflect on 'a moment in time', real or imaginery. For example, imagine a walk in the park and a moment when you watch someone kicking up leaves or finding an object. Tell the group they can use this 'moment' to inspire an image or scene within a box. Invite them to re-create the moment by making a collage or abstract interpretation, using collected or found objects – show any sample available on boxed art, and help people with ideas. Explain that they can use the box as a frame, which will then become an integral part of the work. The boxes can be displayed on walls or standing on plinths, tables or shelves. Discuss the outcome with members, and celebrate the ways in which the artists in the group have interpreted their 'moments'.

Alternative

Use recycled cardboard, wooden boxes and shoeboxes in a session. These will make cost-effective 'frames', and will hold three-dimensional objects to create interesting and sculptural artwork. Suggest that group members identify new themes that they would like to use to inspire work in these boxes.

Comments

Boxed frames can be purchased from art and craft outlets or be hand-made by individuals. Instruct people to attach mirror brackets to the back of the box, before starting their work, if they want to mount the final piece on a wall or display board. Work within the boxes can be three-dimensional, and could include small sculptures or mobiles.

Speechmark

Aim

* **To create a 'Pandora's box', working with negative aspects of art in therapeutic ways.**

Materials

* **Art Resource Box**
* **Shoe boxes or flat A4 boxes**
* **Cards cut to fit inside the boxes**
* **Any information on Pandora's box – search encyclopaedias, the library and the internet.**

Method

Explain to the group, and discuss briefly, the story behind Pandora's box. Point out that Pandora was given a box and forbidden to open it, but, overcome by curiosity, she opened the box, releasing the evils that were to plague humanity. Once all the evils had been released, only 'hope' remained in the box. Invite people to draw or write on the cards (quickly and spontaneously) any negative thoughts they have about themselves as artists, or art in general. (Keep this exercise anonymous.)

When group members have finished drawing and writing, instruct them to place the cards in the box. Ask the group to decide what to do with the box. Offer several options: to throw it away, bury it, or to open it and explore its contents. If the group decides to open the box, go through the cards anonymously. Acknowledge and validate the negative thoughts, and challenge the group to find ways in which to turn these thoughts around into something positive and hopeful – even if it is a decision to eliminate the thought by tearing up the card! Ask people to try again, redrawing or writing down positive and hopeful thoughts about themselves as artists, or art in general, and filling the box with these thoughts to refer to as required.

Alternatives

1 Various themes can be used with this project, to enable people to explore the negative as well as the positive thoughts they have, not only in art, but in other areas of their lives. For example group members could explore skills and thoughts about self-image, or being a mother, cook, employee, partner, musician, or friend. They can draw the images or use pictures cut from magazines to illustrate thoughts and words that they choose to place in the box.

Pandora's Box *(cont'd)*

2 Invite group members to keep and collect their most hated or disliked artworks, and store these in Pandora's box, rather than throw them away. From time to time, open the box, select a piece of work and see if the work can be changed or developed into a more positive and acceptable piece by the artist.

Comments

Many artists who have experienced trauma, or living with mental illness, use art as an expressive tool to release negative or harmful thoughts. Pandora's box has the potential to be a therapeutic vehicle to carry artists through difficult times and deal with negative thoughts creatively. Individual boxes can be made and kept confidential, or shared with someone the artist trusts.

Speechmark

Aims

* **To encourage group members to collect and store recycled materials for future use in art activities**
* **To enable group members to be creative and resourceful.**

Materials

* **A large box, or stacking boxes, to store the collection of 'junk' materials, ideas and information**
* **Self-adhesive labels**
* **Marker pens to label boxes.**

Method

This project offers an opportunity for the facilitator and group members to collect useful resources for art activities at a very low cost. Spend time with the group identifying the materials they need for activities and projects. Ask them to consider which materials they enjoy working with, and that can be collected and stored in a junk box, preferably at no cost to the group – make sure that the suggestions are realistic! Materials such as scrap paper, fabrics, string, shoelaces, corrugated paper, nuts and bolts and any other 'junk' will prove useful. As a group, decide how these will be collected and stored, and allocate tasks to individuals or small teams within the group.

Alternative

Encourage group members to have a go at creating junk sculptures and collages with the objects they have collected.

Comments

A junk box can harbour many groupwork ideas and inspirations for future artworks – for example, a simple design on scrap material can influence a piece of work. This can be a therapeutic art intervention for the conservationist and saves on the budget! It is important to have the appropriate glue and a base to work from if using heavier materials for collage and sculptures. Do some research on this if necessary, and be aware of the risk assessments and guidelines needed when using potentially hazardous substances or materials.

Random

Aim

* **To encourage teamwork, and create a collective presentation of work by the group.**

Materials

* **Art Resource Box**
* **A4 boxes (not too deep)**
* **Collection of work, A4 in size, by group members.**

Method

Encourage group members to select some of their favourite work. Photocopy/ reduce (or scan and print) the work to A4, and place the random collection in an A4 box. Ask the group to give the box a title if desired. People can continue to work randomly on other themes and ideas to produce A4 sized work. Have the group set a time-scale, and limit the number of works in each box, if desired. If feasible, suggest that people copy each work several times, so that each member of the team can have a copy of the box.

Alternative

Offer the group an opportunity to create a random box of smaller images and artwork, designed on blank postcards stored in index boxes. These, and other work, can also be scanned and stored on computer, if desired.

Comments

This is a positive way to encourage group members to share work, and have a means to remember and celebrate their time together. A random box can be a collection of work on a specific theme, or created randomly and spontaneously by individuals or groups. Boxes can include prints, photographs, collage, sketching, rubbings, paintings and small objects.

Speechmark

Art and Words

Creative writing, poetry and the expressive use of words are art forms in themselves. When used in conjunction with images and objects, they can become powerful communication tools. For people with learning disabilities or communication needs, art and words can offer an effective total communication and person-centred approach to self-awareness and expression.

Aims

* **To use observation skills and words to describe what group members see.**
* **To create images, and develop the imagination, by using these words as a source of inspiration.**

Materials

* **Art Resource Box**
* **Flipchart and marker pens**
* **Objects for still life drawing – for example, plants, a bowl of fruit, colourful silk scarves crumpled together.**

Method

Assemble a still life presentation for the group, and invite members to spend time observing it closely. Encourage them to look at the shapes, colours, tones, textures and patterns. After a few minutes, ask people to call out words spontaneously, while they are observing the still life – for example, 'green', 'leaves', 'red', 'rose', 'silk', 'pink', 'ballerina', 'light' or 'soft'.

Write the words on the flipchart, or large sheet of paper attached to the wall or board. (Do simple line drawings if there are people in the group who are unable to read the words.) Next, remove the objects from sight, and invite people to create a picture using only the words on the flipchart to inspire their work. Reassure them that the final image does not have to look like the original still life.

Alternative

Suggest to group members that they use words only in sketchbooks (or recorded on to tape), to avoid reproducing exactly what is seen, and to encourage more abstract and imaginative dimensions. They can draw or paint from the words later, when back in their studio/workspace. This can be done in any situation, and is useful to artists who shy away from sketching in public, but do not mind making written notes.

Comments

This exercise encourages use of observation and descriptive skills. Removing the objects and using only words challenges the artist to call on memory and imagination when creating an artwork. This can be very stimulating and rewarding.

The Art Activity Manual © Marylyn Cropley 2004

Aim

* **To create images that illustrate/complement the written word**

Materials

* **Art Resource Box**
* **A4 ring binder files and clear plastic sleeves**
* **A4 cards, or thick paper**
* **Magazines with pictures to cut up for collage**
* **Examples of short stories or poems.**

Method

Work with the group to write a short story, together or individually. Have ideas prepared to inspire or prompt the creative writing exercise within the group (or samples of work by other artists). Encourage people to be as descriptive as possible, and as realistic or fantastic as desired. Tell them to write freely: there are no set rules for this exercise, within reason! Ask people to choose a favourite piece, and suggest that they try illustrating some aspect of the written work. They should use A4 paper for their writing and illustrations, so that they can place the finished work in clear plastic sleeves in A4 files, to present a creative book format.

Alternative

Stretch the imagination by reading out an unfinished sentence, to be completed and illustrated by the group – for example, 'Looking out the window I see … ', 'Mary stepped on to the magic carpet, and … ', 'The antique shop was filled with treasures … ', and 'John picked up a glowing … '

Comments

This activity offers a humorous and relaxing atmosphere, in which group members work together in a non-competitive and non-threatening way. Books can hold random or themed work by the group, as a collective enterprise, or individual projects. Words need not be made into poems or short stories: single words, or short phrases within an illustration can be used.

Haiku and Art

Aim

* **To experience using haiku to inspire creative writing and illustrations.**

Materials

* **Art Resource Box**
* **Information on haiku (optional)**
* **Ideas to inspire haiku**
* **Notebooks.**

Method

Take the group for a walk, encouraging them to study the local environment. Suggest that they take the notebooks with them, and spend some time listing words to describe what they see literally. For example, a woodland area might inspire words such as 'autumn', 'leaves', 'trees', 'tall', 'clustered', 'stretching out', 'together', 'wooden', 'green' or 'mystical'. When the group returns to the workspace, or when out and about, ask them to use the words to create a short poem in the haiku style. Explain what is needed, and point out that the words do not rhyme!

Inform the group that the format for the haiku consists of three lines, one under the other, with each line containing syllables that graduate in the following way: seven syllables in the first line, five in the second line and seven in the third line. The haiku should include a season word ('summer', 'leaves', 'blossom') to indicate the time it was written, for example:

Trees in autumn, leaves abound
Waving in the wind –
What secrets lie within you?

Inspire the group to use the haiku to create realistic, abstract, imaginative or mystical illustrations.

Alternatives

1 Use haiku in sketchbooks – this can be addictive!
2 Look at creative writing styles in other cultures/countries, and ask group members to create and illustrate their own work in these styles.

Comments

Some people may find it difficult to grasp the concept of syllables initially. Encourage group members to assist each other, and have samples of Japanese haiku to show the group.

Speechmark

Aim

* **To offer an opportunity for group members to have discussions on different aspects of art, which will increase knowledge, vocabulary, awareness and appreciation of art.**

Materials

* **Books, videos, slides and tapes with information on any aspect of art that may be of interest or introduce new dimensions and knowledge of art to the group.**
* **Encourage people to research and bring in resources and ideas for discussion, including their own work.**

Method

Using the books, videos, and slides as prompts, invite the group to talk about and appreciate an area of art that interests or challenges them – they might chose famous artists, or art styles such as impressionism, cubism or modern art. Encourage people to enjoy exploring and appreciating art from as many different perspectives as possible.

Alternative

Encourage group members to visit galleries, artists' studios and foreign lands where possible (individually, as a group, or with friends and relatives) to widen their knowledge and appreciation.

Comments

Keep the activity positive and lively. Some artists have high expectations of themselves, tending to compare themselves with, and trying to live up to, what they perceive to be the expectations of others. This can dull the senses and appreciation of art as a creative, rich and fulfilling experience. Encourage the group to indulge in a good debate, to challenge self and others, widen horizons, and remember why they appreciated art in the first place! Keep the language simple, introduce new words, and use a variety of visual prompts to support those who have difficulty in speaking out. Ensure they have some input, even if just to point at a favourite picture from a collection.

Art and Music

This project considers music as a source of inspiration to develop art projects for individuals or groups. Many artists, such as Paul Klee, were profoundly influenced by music, and created styles and challenges for themselves through their love and appreciation of music.

Visual art is only a fragment of sensory art, and music adds an exciting and creative dimension for any striving, imaginative and dynamic artist. Music touches the emotions and soothes the soul. It allows a natural, sensitive and therapeutic approach to art, and, in turn, stimulates other senses.

Free Expression to Music

Aim

* **To offer the opportunity to create images freely and randomly, inspired by music.**

Materials

* **Art Resource Box**
* **Music (CDs or tapes brought in by group members) and a CD/tape player.**

Method

Begin the session by playing some soft, relaxing music to the group. Invite members to paint or draw spontaneously to the music when they feel ready. Suggest that they use colours, shapes and lines freely and randomly. People can work in small groups, or individually. Enable the group to enjoy the process and the music! Ask someone in the group to select another piece of music, when everyone has finished, and ask the group to try the same exercise to another style of music. Observe the difference in the work. Suggest that group members try a variety of music and sounds, including people's favourites. Ask why these were preferred, and how the choice of music enhanced or inspired the work.

Alternatives

1 Suggest that people have a go at painting or drawing to music blindfolded, if they would like to.
2 Invite the group to listen to songs, and visualise a scene to paint or draw.
3 Hold a session to encourage group members to begin, and develop, a sketchbook inspired by music.

Comments

Painting to music, without analysing the outcome or process, can be very therapeutic. Use this activity as a relaxation exercise. People can frame and display their favourite images, and these can be viewed when listening to the same or similar music.

Music, Words and Art

Aim

* **To create images from words inspired by music.**

Materials

* **Art Resource Box**
* **A variety of music (tapes or CDs) and a tape/CD player**
* **Sketchbooks.**

Method

Arrange for the group to listen to a piece of music for three to five minutes. Then ask them to write a list of words that come to mind spontaneously, inspired by the music they have just heard – for example, 'soft', 'hard', 'angry', 'happy', 'red', 'blue', 'caves', 'water', or 'birds'. Encourage them to experiment with the words collected, and make sketches inspired by these words. Suggest that they have a go at creating a picture, using the words, sketches and music for reference.

Alternative

Ask people to try writing their own songs to music, or select words from favourite songs, and paint scenes inspired by these words.

Comments

Music and words can help to conjure up inspiring images to work with. They titillate and inspire the imagination. Words from music can also help to trigger or 'kick-start' an idea when the imagination wanes, or motivation is at its weakest.

This page may be photocopied for instructional use only. *The Art Activity Manual* © Marylyn Cropley 2004

Speechmark

Aim

* **To work with colours and music, to stretch the imagination.**

Materials

* **Art Resource Box**
* **A 'colourful' collection of music (tapes or CDs) and a tape/CD player**
* **A collection of coloured items, such as scarves, fabrics or colour cards.**

Method

Instruct the group to listen to a piece of music carefully. If possible, ask people to close their eyes, and try to visualise colours while listening to the music. Then encourage them to create images in their heads, real or abstract, using only the colours inspired by the music. Some people may find it difficult to visualise or imagine colours, so have a collection of scarves, fabrics or colour cards ready for people to select spontaneously, while listening to the music. Ask them to hold and look at the items chosen, then close their eyes and try to visualise these colours while continuing to listen to the music. People can then have a go at painting what they have visualised. They can use the scarves and colour cards as a reference, if needed.

Alternative

If the above exercise proves difficult for the group initially, have a session where the group can listen to a variety of sounds and music. Choose one piece of music with the group, then ask them to close their eyes and listen to the music for a few minutes. Invite the group to call out the names of colours, randomly as they spring to mind, while listening to the music. Write these colours down for the group on a large sheet of paper, and ask group members to paint the colours on the paper, next to the appropriate words. The group can then use the colours to create an image inspired by the music, either individually or collectively.

Comments

Be aware that some people are colour-blind, and enable them to share the colours they see with the group in a non-judgemental and appreciative way. Working with artists who are colour-blind can inspire others to see colours from a new and exciting perspective!

Images and Music

Aim

* To use the imagination, and create images from music selected by the group.

Materials

* Art Resource Box
* Music CDs or tapes (encourage group members to bring some in), and a CD/tape player
* Bring in music that depicts a certain theme or concept, such as the sea, people in love, or a walk on the beach.

Method

Select a piece of music for the group, and invite them to listen to the piece for a few minutes. Ask people to close their eyes, and try to visualise an image or scene inspired by the music – for example, landscapes, people walking by the sea or dancing on the waves, caves, rocks, waves crashing against a shipwreck, or clear blue skies.

Encourage the group to dwell on the images in detail, and to try to visualise and memorise what they 'see'. Play the music for as long as they need, then invite the group to try to reproduce the specific images in art form, with as much detail as they can remember. They can draw sketches as they listen to the music, as a reference for the final piece.

Alternative

Encourage people to bring in their own music, and practise keeping a record of the music and the images that were inspired in a sketchbook, for future reference.

Comments

Listening to music can conjure up all kinds of images and feelings, both soothing and harsh. Be prepared for emotions to manifest themselves in different ways within the group. Offer support, and do not allow any person to feel pressured to participate if they are not ready to do so, nor 'in the mood'. However, most will find this experience, and the sharing of pictures, therapeutic and stimulating.

Using Different Surfaces

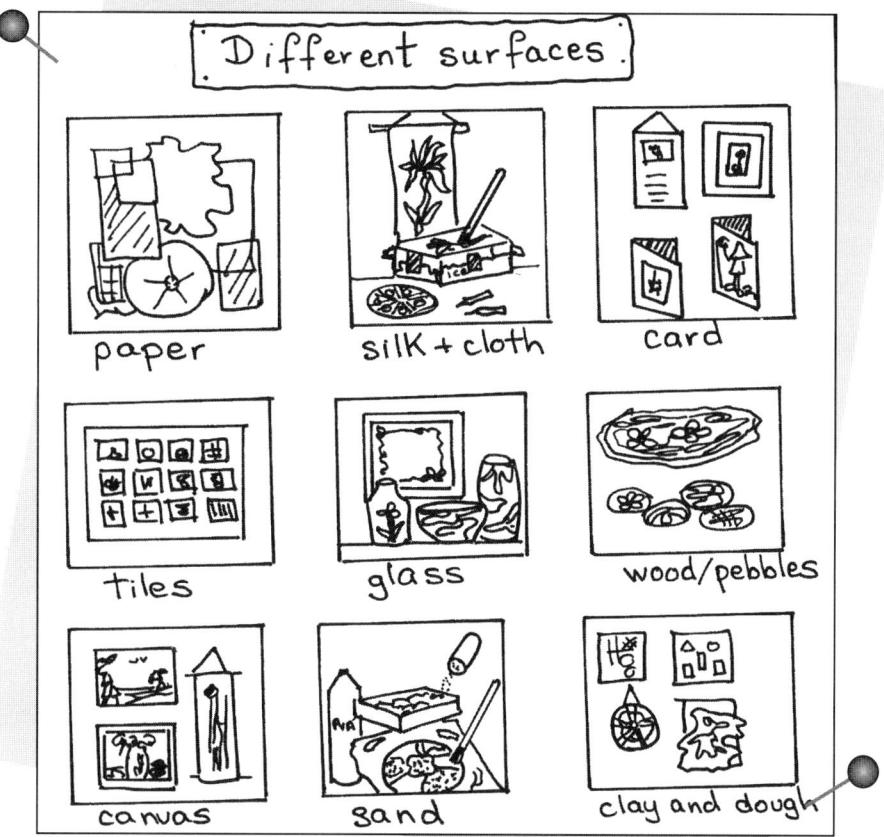

Different surfaces

paper
silk + cloth
card
tiles
glass
wood/pebbles
canvas
sand
clay and dough

Some artists discover a surface on which to create their images and stick to it – for example, watercolour and acrylic on paper or canvas. Others explore further, and create images on walls, inside caves, on ceramics, wood, and within nature itself in the form of land art. Some continue on a quest for the perfect surface! The scope is wide, diverse and exciting. Creating images on different surfaces can be challenging and stimulating for any artist. Every artist deserves to treat themselves to a new experience and surface, and to have fun doing so, shamelessly! So go ahead, and enjoy the following projects!

Paper

Aim

* **To enable group members to experiment with, and experience the process of, creating images on a variety of textured papers.**

Materials

* **Art Resource Box**
* **A collection of different papers, such as acrylic, watercolour, blotting, tissue and wallpaper**
* **Magazines to cut up.**

Method

Invite the group to choose from the selection of papers on offer. Experiment by using different paper to paint or draw on. Help them to find preferences and explore different ways to work with them. They can stick various papers on top of each other, and try painting or printing abstractly, using different colours and tones on the layers. Encourage people to experiment, and see what happens!

Alternative

Much can be achieved when using paper in conventional or unconventional ways: encourage group members to collect ideas and have fun experimenting. Suggest that they try using ink, dropped randomly on blotting paper, or watercolour paints splashed on absorbent paper, to create different effects. They can make collages using paper, or create textured surfaces, either by layering paper, or covering a flat board with papier mâché.

Comments

Offer an opportunity for people to have a go at making paper, or invite someone to work with the group on a paper-making project.

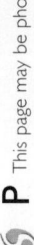

Aim

* **To create images on fabrics using silk paints.**

Materials

* **Silk paints**
* **White silk or cotton fabric squares**
* **Embroidery rings for frames, or square/rectangular plastic ice-cream containers**
* **Instructions for using silk paints.**

Method

Ask group members to stretch the silk or cotton fabrics on to the embroidery rings, or over the open top of an ice-cream container (hold the edges of the fabric down, and stick this to the sides of the container with masking tape). People can paint designs and images straight on to the fabric using the silk paints, or draw the outline in pencil before stretching the fabrics on to the frames. Check the instructions that come with the paints, and do a brief demonstration if necessary, before asking the group to start. Enable the group to frame the finished work, or create silk books or cards.

Alternatives

1 Silk paints can be expensive, but are worth a try. Alternatively, suggest that group members use acrylic paints instead: they are durable, and can be used on most textiles.
2 Encourage people to have a go at decorating T-shirts, bags, shoes, cushion covers or wall hangings – the list is endless!

Comments

Unwanted, disposable contact lens cases (the flat type) are excellent as palettes for using and storing silk paints. Ask anyone who wears contact lenses to save the cases for these sessions!

Cardboard

Aim

* **To experience creating artwork on surfaces made from cardboard.**

Materials

* **Art Resource Box**
* **Various kinds of cardboard, including corrugated card, scrap and collage materials.**

Method

Card is useful for collage work, and any artwork which needs a firm base. It can be folded to make greeting cards, or cut into large squares to form a mount on which to display artworks. Explore and consider the many uses of card with the group. Ask people to come up with ideas, or research the ways in which card is used commercially and by individual artists. Try out some of the ideas collected.

Alternatives

1   Use corrugated card for making layered print blocks or raised panels.
2   Suggest that the group members try some collage work using different kinds of cardboard they have collected over the period of a week.

Comments

Do further research, with the group, on the different ways cardboard is used in art.

Speechmark

Aim

* **To offer people an opportunity to create designs and images on tiled surfaces.**

Materials

* **Acrylic paints**
* **Brushes, and varnish or PVA glue**
* **White ceramic tiles**
* **Hooks or tape to attach tiles to the wall (optional)**
* **Square wooden bases, slightly larger than tiles, on which to attach them for display**
* **Strong glue suitable for using with wood or ceramics.**

Method

Agree on a theme for the project with group members – for example, nature, shapes, colours or patterns. Invite the group to draw images or patterns on to the tiles, or offer the use of templates to help those who lack the confidence to do this freehand. Suggest that they decorate the tiles with acrylic paints. When they are dry, recommend that people glaze each tile with varnish or PVA glue (optional). Tiles can be displayed on walls, or as a montage on a wooden backing. Tiles can also be used as place mats for cold food.

Alternatives

1 Group members' ideas and designs can be transferred on to bathroom or kitchen tiles, or several tiles displayed on a wall in the garden as a form of installation.
2 People can have a go at painting tiles in different colours and use them broken into pieces, to create mosaics. Self-adhesive mosaic tiles are also available, and may be easier for some people to use.

Comments

There are ceramic paints on the market (look in DIY stores) that can be tried with groups. Check the instructions first, to make sure the paint is suitable for your group. Exercise caution when purchasing or using any glue or broken ceramic tiles for the group. Ensure that group members are aware of, and are observing, any relevant health and safety guidelines.

Glass

Aim

* **To enable group members to enjoy the experience of painting and decorating glass surfaces.**

Materials

* **Glass paints or acrylics**
* **Instructions on using glass paints**
* **Tracing paper**
* **Masking tape**
* **A selection of glass jars, vases, small mirrors and bowls**
* **Pictures and ideas to inspire**
* **Hairdryer to speed up drying (optional).**

Method

Invite the group to create designs and images on paper. They can then paint these directly on to the glass surface with the glass or acrylic paints. If people find it difficult to draw on the glass freehand, trace the image on to tracing paper, and stick the paper inside the glass jar or bowl with masking tape. They can then draw over the image where it shows through the glass with the outliner from the glass paint set, or use a permanent black marker pen if using acrylic paints. When the outline has dried, instruct them to fill in the colours.

Alternative

Hold a session where people can design and make gifts for a specific person, by decorating a vase, bowl or mirror. Ask them to talk about the gift, why they chose the item for the person, and the thoughts behind their design.

Comments

Remind the group to wait for the outliner to dry before painting in the colours, unless they are happy with a smudged effect, or that the paints may run into each other (this can also be quite effective). Instruct the group to exercise caution when using glass paints and glass, and be extra vigilant. Check that group members are aware of risk assessments and health and safety procedures. Water-based glass paints do not need baking, and are ideal for painting on surfaces that do not need washing; however, oven-baked paints are more durable. This is a popular activity: many a jam jar decorated in this way still holds a small cluster of daffodils years later!

16

PART III: USING DIFFERENT SURFACES

Pebbles

Aim

* **To enable group members to enjoy the experience of painting and decorating pebbles.**

Materials

* **Acrylic or poster paints**
* **PVA glue or varnish**
* **Large, smooth, clean pebbles**
* **Ideas and images for creating illustrations to draw and paint on pebbles**
* **Magazines and photographs to cut up for collage on pebbles.**

Method

Instruct the group to ensure that the pebbles have fairly flat and clean surfaces, before beginning to work on them. Invite them to have a go at painting designs and images, real or abstract, on the pebbles with acrylic paints. Suggest that they cut out unusual and exotic pictures from magazines if desired, and paste these on to the pebbles. Recommend that they keep the designs simple, and that they glaze over the collage with some acrylic paint and PVA glue mixture. If not using PVA glue, they may want to varnish the pebble when finished.

Alternatives

1   To begin with, suggest that group members paint lots of small/medium sized pebbles, to practise and gain confidence in handling this surface. When finished, the colourful pebbles can be placed in a glass bowl, with a candle set in the middle (safely encased in foil or glass), laid on the compost surface of a potted plant, or displayed in other creative ways suggested by the group.
2   People can display favourite photographs (photocopied and cut out) or use their favourite dried flowers or leaves. Paste these on to large pebbles, and varnish to preserve the work.
3   Invite the group to make decorative pebbles, to be displayed individually, or set in cement in the garden as a mosaic.

Comments

Pebbles are fun to decorate, but it can be difficult to know which images to select without the result looking 'cheap' and 'tacky'. However, encourage people to experiment, and enjoy the process, before reaching a satisfactory outcome.

16

Wood

Aim

* **To explore using different wood surfaces.**

Materials

* **Acrylic paints**
* **PVA and wood glue**
* **Varnish**
* **A selection of different types of wood, such as balsa wood, hardboard, MDF (cut into small squares), or found wood (tree trunks cut into slices)**
* **Natural objects for making collages, such as leaves, nuts, seeds and lentils.**

Method

Ask each person to select a piece of wood. Suggest people spend a little time looking at the wood before deciding what image to create, and which piece to use. Instruct them to draw or paint directly on to the wood, or make a collage using natural objects. Use PVA or wood glue to stick the collage on to the wood, and finish with a couple of coats of varnish or PVA glue. Suggest to the group that the finished picture can be hung as it is, or mounted on another piece of wood.

Alternatives

1 Wood can provide an exciting and challenging base to work on. Natural wood, such as slices of tree trunks, can be exhibited both indoors and outdoors. Suggest that people design a house name or number on natural wood, and hang this on a tree or the side of their house.

2 Have a session using only balsa wood. This wood is soft and lightweight and images can be impressed into it for textured effects, then painted over. Light and colourful mobiles can also be made from smaller balsa wood shapes.

3 Encourage people to collect and recycle unwanted wooden chopping boards, placemats or trays: they can sand off the old surfaces and repaint the objects with images and patterns.

Comments

Wood can be an exciting and challenging material to work on. However, some people in the group will need more input from the facilitator than others. It may also be necessary for the facilitator to check the materials used, before the group meets, to ensure there are no pieces of wood with splinters in them, or that the wood is not unsuitable and unprepared for painting, thus avoiding any frustration and disappointment in the session.

Canvas

Aim

* **To enable group members to experience painting and drawing on stretched canvas.**

Materials

* **Art Resource Box**
* **Ready-stretched canvas on lightweight frames**
* **Small eye hooks and string for hanging canvases.**

Method

Encourage people to have fun experimenting with painting on canvas. Suggest that they draw images directly on to the canvas with pencils, paint or charcoal, or experiment with ideas in a sketchbook first. They can paint, using acrylic or oil pastels, or make quick charcoal sketches that can be left as they are, or painted over if desired. Any mistakes can be painted over with white acrylic paint and repainted.

When finished, assist people to hang their work. They can do this by screwing eye hooks in the back of the wooden frame of the canvas, one third of the way down on either side, and stretching the string taut across the back of the canvas, between the two eye hooks. People can then hang their pictures without needing to frame them.

Alternative

Ask group members to have a go at stretching their own canvas. Instructions can be obtained in art books from the library, or you could invite a local artist/tutor in to do a demonstration or workshop.

Comments

Ready-made stretched canvases on wooden frames (with the surface primed and ready for use) can be purchased at reasonable prices from art shops or discount stores. Lightweight, stretched canvases on frames are useful outdoors and can be re-used when painted over with white paint or primer.

It is well worth offering the group members an opportunity to try oil paints on canvas, but bear in mind that oils take time to dry thoroughly. Consider inviting an artist to do a demonstration for the group, or to teach a few sessions on working with oils.

Aim

❊ **To offer the group opportunities to work with a tactile surface such as sand, in innovative ways.**

Materials

❊ **Card and paper**
❊ **Coloured sands, or white sand (from pet shops, DIY stores, or art and craft shops)**
❊ **PVA glue**
❊ **Pencils**
❊ **Acrylic paints or coloured inks, if using white sand only.**

Method

Invite people to draw an image on card or paper – they can trace or transfer images on to card by drawing over carbon paper, if necessary. Instruct them to fill inside the lines with PVA glue (fairly thickly), and sprinkle sand generously over the glued area. They then need to push the sand gently into the corners with fingers and shake off the surplus on to paper. (Save the surplus sand to use again.) Suggest that they experiment with different patterns, colours, images or designs.

Alternatives

1　Sand can be used loosely in trays. Invite group members to enjoy the tactile experience by encouraging them to create lines and patterns on the surface of sand that is placed in shallow trays or cardboard boxes – the sand may need to be dampened slightly.

2　Go to the beach with the group, or build larger sandboxes together for more space to work in, to create land art designs and images.

3　Give the group salt instead of sand to work with. Colour the salt by pouring some on a sheet of white paper, then roll coloured chalk firmly over the salt several times until the salt changes colour. Pour the coloured salt into small containers to use or store as required.

Comments

Ensure that there is adequate space and provision for working with a group that is using a fairly messy medium – it can get into eyes and mouths, and everywhere else! Hold the group responsible for the way they work with this medium, and for clearing up afterwards.

Aim

* **To enable people to experiment with, and enjoy using, clay surfaces to create a piece of artwork.**

Materials

* **Art Resource Box**
* **Clay or self-hardening clay**
* **Rolling pin and tools for cutting and drawing on clay – for example, knitting needles, toothpicks, lollipop sticks, old knives and forks, large paper-clips**
* **Sandpaper and small sponges.**
* **Unwanted rolls of wallpaper or hessian cloths**
* **Kitchen rolls**
* **Templates, such as ceramic tiles or squares of card or wood.**

Method

Give each group member a piece of clay, and have them place this on a piece of wallpaper or a hessian cloth – this will stop the clay sticking to the table. Ask each person to roll out the clay to a desired thickness to make square tile shapes. They can use the ceramic tiles or other templates, if desired, to cut out the shape. Next, they need to draw patterns or images on the clay surface, using the tools provided. When the clay is dry, they can smooth any rough edges gently, using a damp sponge or sandpaper. Invite people to paint the clay surface with acrylic or poster paints. When completely dry, they can varnish the work with PVA glue or varnish. The finished work can be hung on walls, glued on to a large wooden board, or displayed on a plate stand. Discuss with the group how they wish to do this, and assist where necessary.

Alternatives

1   Suggest that group members make a montage or mosaic display, with large or small clay shapes glued on to wood or hardboard backings.
2   Instruct members to make clay tiles with textured surfaces, and use these as printing blocks when dry. (If using tiles as printing blocks, do not glaze the surface.)

Comments

Self-hardening clay is quick, clean and easy to use, and does not need to be fired in a kiln. However, any clay will do, although some may need to be painted and varnished if unsuitable for the kiln. If a kiln is available, the clay can be fired and glazed to create interesting textures and colours. However, do seek appropriate support, advice and guidance on how to use kilns and prepare clay for firing!

Aim

* **To enable people to make dough, and experience working with this medium.**

Materials

* **Art Resource Box**
* **Plain white flour**
* **Salt**
* **Oil (optional, but it prevents dough from sticking)**
* **Water**
* **Large bowls**
* **Rolling pins**
* **Wooden or plastic boards**
* **Measuring cup (any size, depending on the amount of dough needed)**
* **Square templates or ceramic tiles**
* **Implements for cutting dough and adding textures or lines to the surface**
* **Any books on dough art and craft**
* **Access to an oven.**

Method

Explain to the group that they will be making dough surfaces to work on. Ask volunteers in the group to make the dough. They will need to mix two level cups of plain flour with one level cup of cooking salt. Then get them to mix the dried ingredients together, and add three-quarters of a cup of water and two teaspoons cooking oil (optional). Next they can bind together and knead the dough mix for 10 minutes (this is important!) on a board. Share out the dough, then ask people to roll out their piece to the desired thickness, and cut it to shape by eye, or using ceramic tiles or templates.

Ask the group to create textures and patterns on the dough surface, using the implements available. Help the group to bake the tiles as soon as they are finished, to prevent edges from drying out. They will need to cook at 120°C (250°F), and be baked until the dough is solid (approximately eight or nine hours – less time is needed when using a fan-assisted oven). Leave the tiles in the oven

This page may be photocopied for instructional use only. *The Art Activity Manual* © Marylyn Cropley 2004

Speechmark

until cool. When ready, ask group members to paint the surfaces with acrylic or poster paints, and leave to dry for approximately 24 hours, before varnishing with polyurethane varnish. Suggest they varnish the back of the tile first and, after 12 hours, varnish the front.

Alternative

Ask the group to come up with suggestions for using artworks produced on dough. A good example would be to make decorations for the Christmas tree.

Comments

Remind group members to exercise caution with varnishes. Ensure ventilation is good, and tell the group they *must not* re-cook the tiles once varnished, as fumes from the varnish may be toxic and inflammable.

Inspiration from Well-known Artists

Gaining insight and inspiration by studying the work of other artists can be fruitful and stimulating. The idea is to use this experience as a trigger or springboard to finding and developing personal styles and preferences. This project can cover a whole year or more of activities based around other artists, as there are hundreds of them out there to discover and explore! Where possible, visit galleries, museums and studios that exhibit, and bring people closer to, the original work and experiences of the artist involved. Also study the people and places known to these artists, as many were influenced by other artists, in their turn – which opens doors to further explorations!

Matisse – 'The Snail'

Aims

* **To enable the group to gain inspiration from the work of Henri Matisse (1869–1954)**
* **To work as a team to create a collage on a similar theme and style to that of 'The Snail'.**

Materials

* **Art Resource Box**
* **Opaque watercolour or gouache paints**
* **Large sheets of paper (white)**
* **Pictures of animals (simple outlines)**
* **Books, pictures or videos on Henri Matisse.**

Method

Spend some time exploring the work of Matisse with the group, and looking at 'The Snail' in particular. Ask the group to consider how 'The Snail' was made: Matisse, confined to bed due to ill health, gave instructions to assistants to paint large sheets of paper with gouache, choosing the colours himself. He then cut shapes from the papers, and directed his assistants to paste the shapes on to white paper to form 'The Snail'.

Do a similar exercise with the group. Invite someone from the group to 'be Matisse', to select the colours for others to paint, suggest how to cut out the shapes, and to give instructions on where to paste the shapes on the sheet of white paper. Try other creatures, such as a giraffe, lion, snake or butterfly, and take it in turns to 'be Matisse'.

Alternative

Hold a session where group members can experiment with paints other than gouache, or create collages with coloured tissue paper.

Comments

This activity involves all participants in the group, especially those with limited movement. They can participate by selecting the animal and colours, and by giving the instructions. Matisse was fascinated with decorative textiles covered in exotic patterns. He used bold colours and shapes, and also experimented with pointillism, primitive art, colour, shape, form and light. Other artists who used collage and primitive art, and experimented with shapes and colours, include Georges Bracque, Pablo Picasso, Ben Nicholson, Paul Cézanne and Paul Gauguin.

Van Gogh – 'Still Life'

Aims

* To explore the works of Vincent van Gogh (1853–1890)
* To offer the opportunity for group members to paint flowers in the style of Van Gogh, and experience using oils or acrylic paints thickly and expressively.

Materials

* Art Resource Box
* Oil paints (optional)
* Acrylic paints (include various shades of yellow and brown)
* Sunflowers (real or artificial), or other yellow flowers
* Pottery vase to hold flowers
* Canvas or paper for acrylic paints
* Information on, and books showing pictures by, Van Gogh – include 'Sunflowers' (1888).

Method

Look at 'Sunflowers' by Van Gogh. Ask the group to consider the way in which he uses paint thickly, and the bold colours and strokes he employs. Study together, the flower pictures he painted, and ask people to have a go at painting the still life flowers in a similar style. Suggest they use a range of yellow and brown tones, and paint thickly and freely with a variety of short or long strokes. Enjoy the process, and see what happens. Explain to the group that the final piece must not look exactly like Van Gogh's!

Alternative

Look at other work by Van Gogh with the group, such as his portraits and landscapes. Invite group members to study his style and approaches to these works, and to try creating their own pictures in a similar style.

Comments

Van Gogh was interested in people and portraits, as well as still life. He also showed emotion and humanity in his work, and is a very colourful and moving artist to study. His work influenced expressionism, fauvism and abstract art. However, there is a sense of realism throughout his works, which complements his desire to paint life as he lived and saw it – another topic for a project, perhaps: to paint life as we live and see it!

Speechmark

Monet – 'Gardens'

Aims

To enable participants to:
* **Explore and study the world of Claude Oscar Monet (1840–1926)**
* **Create a collection of pictures inspired by gardens, and Monet's interpretations of them**
* **Experience and appreciate working on canvas, outdoors with nature.**

Materials

* **Canvas stretched on lightweight wooden frames**
* **Easel (optional)**
* **Portable Art Resources Box with selected media**
* **Information about Claude Monet**
* **An interesting local garden to visit and sketch or paint**
* **Sketchbooks.**

Method

Spend some time looking at the work of Monet with the group. Encourage members to consider the ways in which he captures what he sees, the use of light and colour, and the impressions he creates. Suggest a visit to a garden or a local place of interest – with a lily pond if possible! Encourage participants to have a go at creating an impression of what they see, focusing on the light and colour. If possible, get the group to re-create the same scene at different times of the day or year.

Alternative

If feasible, arrange for the group to visit places that other artists (local or famous) have used as subjects in their paintings and artwork – the aim is to inspire the group just as others have been inspired when visiting Monet's garden and seeing the water lilies and reflections for real!

Comments

Monet appears to enjoy painting people (including cartoon characters), as well as landscapes and nature. He used blocks of colours, emphasising details with light, small brush strokes. It is a challenge to explore and re-create his approach to landscape painting.

This page may be photocopied for instructional use only. *The Art Activity Manual* © Marylyn Cropley 2004

PART III: INSPIRATION FROM WELL-KNOWN ARTISTS

17

Kandinsky – 'Colour, Shapes and Lines'

Aim

* **To enable group members to explore and appreciate the work of Wassily Kandinsky (1866–1944), and to create images inspired by his use of colour, shape, and line.**

Materials

* **Art Resource Box**
* **Oil paints and watercolour inks (optional)**
* **Books with illustrations of work by, and information on, Kandinsky**
* **Canvas stretched on frames or large sketchbooks**
* **Circle templates or compasses and rulers.**

Method

Look at and explore the work of Kandinsky with group members. Encourage them to consider the use of circles, straight lines, detailed patterns and brilliant colours. Ask people to select a shape or pattern from one of Kandinsky's pictures – for example, a circle, line or shape, but not the whole picture! Suggest that they use this shape or pattern to inspire and create their own abstract images. The intention is to not copy Kandinsky's work, but to use circles, lines, patterns and colours in the same dynamic way as he did. Note how his work is sometimes 'loose', and 'fluid', or geometric, with controlled lines and patterns. Ask the group to create work individually or collectively.

Alternatives

1 Ask the group to try creating a work combining abstract and figurative images – for example, recognisable images among abstract colours and shapes.
2 Kandinsky created preliminary sketches, before completing the final piece. Invite the group to work in a similar way, to further enhance and develop their practices.
3 Visit exhibitions/galleries, and seek out work by both Kandinsky and Klee for comparison. Which aspects appeal to the group, and why?

The Art Activity Manual © Marylyn Cropley 2004

17

Comments

Kandinsky's work can be both abstract and figurative. He sometimes used representational images that break away from pure abstract form. Encourage the group to explore his work further and find out about the artist. Other influences and inspirations behind his work appear to be music, a sense of spirituality, and the idea that colours have character and expression of their own. Also explore work by Paul Klee (1879–1940) who, like Kandinsky, was influenced and inspired by music, shapes, patterns and colour. Both artists experimented with new techniques and materials.

Art and Computers

Why use computers for art? Art and communication go hand in hand, as do computers and communication – so why not? Technology has enhanced the materials and tools used by artists, and carries art forward into the twenty-first century. People may fear that computers and digital art will replace traditional art – if not now, then some time in the near future. Looking back over the history of art, and looking around at artists today, we see a healthy combination of traditional and modern art, with movements that complement and add fluidity to art, rather than replacing previous eras. Could not art, like fashion, go full circle? Is digital art becoming the next 'movement' in the history of art?

In recent years, computers have assisted and enhanced opportunities for people with disabilities to communicate and be more creative. Each artist has the power to own a style and create freely. No one can take that away, unless the artist chooses to allow it. To work independently or within the constraints of commercialism, external expectations, and élitism in the art world is a choice. Embracing technology and computers in art is also a choice. Take up the challenge and demonstrate that traditional art and computers can work together, enhancing the work of artists generally, and especially those with special needs. This project offers a tentative introduction to art and computers.

Explore and select the computers, programs, training and support that best suit the group's needs, but be aware of copyright issues – do not copy work belonging to someone else without their permission.

Aim

* **To introduce group members to the concept of using computers to assist and enhance their artwork, to create images, gain inspiration and access information.**

Materials

* **Access to computers, the internet, printers and paper**
* **Basic knowledge of using computers, or someone to assist with this (possibly someone in the group)**
* **Art and graphics computer programs**
* **Computer CDs with clip art, and general information on art, galleries, and artists**
* **A selection of written titles on which to base research – for example, names of famous artists, art movements, or use of colours and textures in art.**

Method

Begin with a general group discussion about what computers have to offer to assist and enhance the work of traditional artists. Topics might include drawing images, using clip art, collecting information on art, learning new art skills and information on gadgets and equipment to assist people with disabilities to use computers creatively. Select a topic with the group, such as an artist (Matisse, Picasso, or Constable) or a sentence or phrase such as 'the use of colour in art'.

Enable group members to research the chosen topic on the computer, using any appropriate CDs or the internet. Use the information acquired to inspire a project, further discussions and artwork, or merely have fun exploring and gaining insight into the world of art.

Alternatives

I Hold a session for group members to look at any local community training opportunities to enable them to develop art and computer skills further – for example Adult Learning computer courses. Research accurate information in advance, or invite people in to speak to the group about the courses on offer.

2 Invite specialist speakers to give demonstrations, or set up projects on computers and art.

Comments

It is important for group facilitators to have some idea of what they are asking people to do, to avoid frustration and delay. Try out the activity first, and be specific about the topics being researched and the tasks set for the group. It may be necessary to direct people to a specific topic and website to begin with, and to practise using this alone before exploring further.

If unable to access computers easily, try the local libraries or colleges to see if they have computer suites available for the public and organisations to use. Encourage group members to use their home computers, if possible, and bring ideas or information in to share with the group. See if it is possible for someone to bring in a laptop computer.

Look out for equipment and tools that are designed for 'hands free' use of computers, and other adaptations that can help someone with a disability to access computers. CD-ROMs and internet sites are available in abundance, with topics covering art and communication with other artists, information on software, resources and equipment, and visits to virtual exhibitions and great art galleries. This is an exciting resource that complements using the local library or borrowing a friend's art book!

Make enquiries to see if it is possible to develop partnerships with local colleges, schools or digital artists, to develop projects. Consider raising funds and obtaining grants to purchase computers and equipment for the group or individual artists. Contact businesses for sponsorship or donation of computer equipment – they may be upgrading equipment, and be happy to give away unwanted computers.

Aims

* **To use computers to enable group members to store, scan and experiment with their own artwork**
* **To offer the opportunity for people to explore and use graphics software.**

Materials

* **Access to computers, scanners (hand-held or flatbed), colour printers, and someone with knowledge of how to use these**
* **A selection of artwork or photographs by group members**
* **Graphics software or a computer art package that will enable group members to scan, enhance or alter artwork, or to draw directly on to the computer using a drawing device.**

Method

Invite group members to scan and store original work on the computer. Use the graphics package for people to 'play around' with an original work, and experiment to see what results can be achieved. Graphics packages allow users to change the original colours, enhance the tones, draw in new lines and shapes, and enlarge or reduce the size of an image. For example, people can enlarge images until only a fraction of the original is seen, and then create another abstract piece with this enlarged section.

Alternative

If possible, hold sessions for group members to learn about using digital cameras and computers. This can further enhance skills and inspire the artist. The photographs produced can help to create a digital sketchbook, which can then be used to create graphics to influence a painting or non-digital piece of art.

Comments

There are many gadgets on the market now that will enable artists with disabilities to use computers for artwork. It is well worth researching this and seeking sponsorship if feasible. For example, it is possible to obtain 'notetakers': these are special pens that enable someone to draw on an A4 sheet of paper, and the images will appear on the computer screen.

Using Computers to Store and Display Work

Aim

* **To create a gallery or portfolio on a computer, by scanning and storing the artwork of group members or an individual artist.**

Materials

* **Access to computer, scanners, colour printer, paper**
* **Digital camera**
* **Artwork and photographs by the group**
* **Software to organise and enhance photographs and scanned images**
* **CDs/discs to store work.**

Method

Look through the artwork with the group, selecting work for the group portfolio or gallery. Help to scan the work on to the computer (hand-held scanners are better for use on large pictures), or take digital photographs of their work. Remember to save the work on CDs or discs. Enable group members to use a digital camera to photograph work by other people, or places visited and artists at work. The digital camera can also be used as a 'digital sketchbook', to record observations and sketches for future work. Enable people to store their work on computer and CDs/discs for future reference, or create slide shows to exhibit on computer or television screens. (NB films taken with conventional cameras can also be stored on CDs when you process your films at most local photographic shops/chemists and mail order film processors.)

Alternatives

1 Personal portfolios and slide shows can be made by individuals to develop an exhibition, send CDs/discs or email to others, or create calendars and cards. This is a flexible way to store, organise and throw away work.

2 If feeling ambitious, the group can create websites and virtual exhibitions to enable them to exhibit and share ideas with a wider audience.

Comments

If any group members wish to explore computers and art further, encourage them to attend local classes or clubs.

Speechmark